insight text guide

Jarrod Sturnieks

Trash

Andy Mulligan

First published in 2024.

Insight Publications Pty Ltd
3/350 Charman Road
Cheltenham VIC 3192
Australia
Tel: +61 3 8571 4950
Email: books@insightpublications.com.au

www.insightpublications.com.au

Andy Mulligan's *Trash* / Jarrod Sturnieks

Jarrod Sturnieks asserts the moral right to be identified as the author of this work.

ISBNs:
9781922771902 (print)
9781922771919 (digital)

Cover design by Hayley Sinnatt
Layout by Melisa Paredes
Edited by Kate McGregor
Proofread by Alison Tealby

Proudly Printed in Australia by Ligare Book Printers.

Insight Publications acknowledges the Traditional Custodians of the Country on which we meet and work, the Boonwurrung People of the Kulin Nation. We pay our respects to their Elders past and present, and extend that respect to all Aboriginal and Torres Strait Islander peoples.

contents

CHARACTER MAP

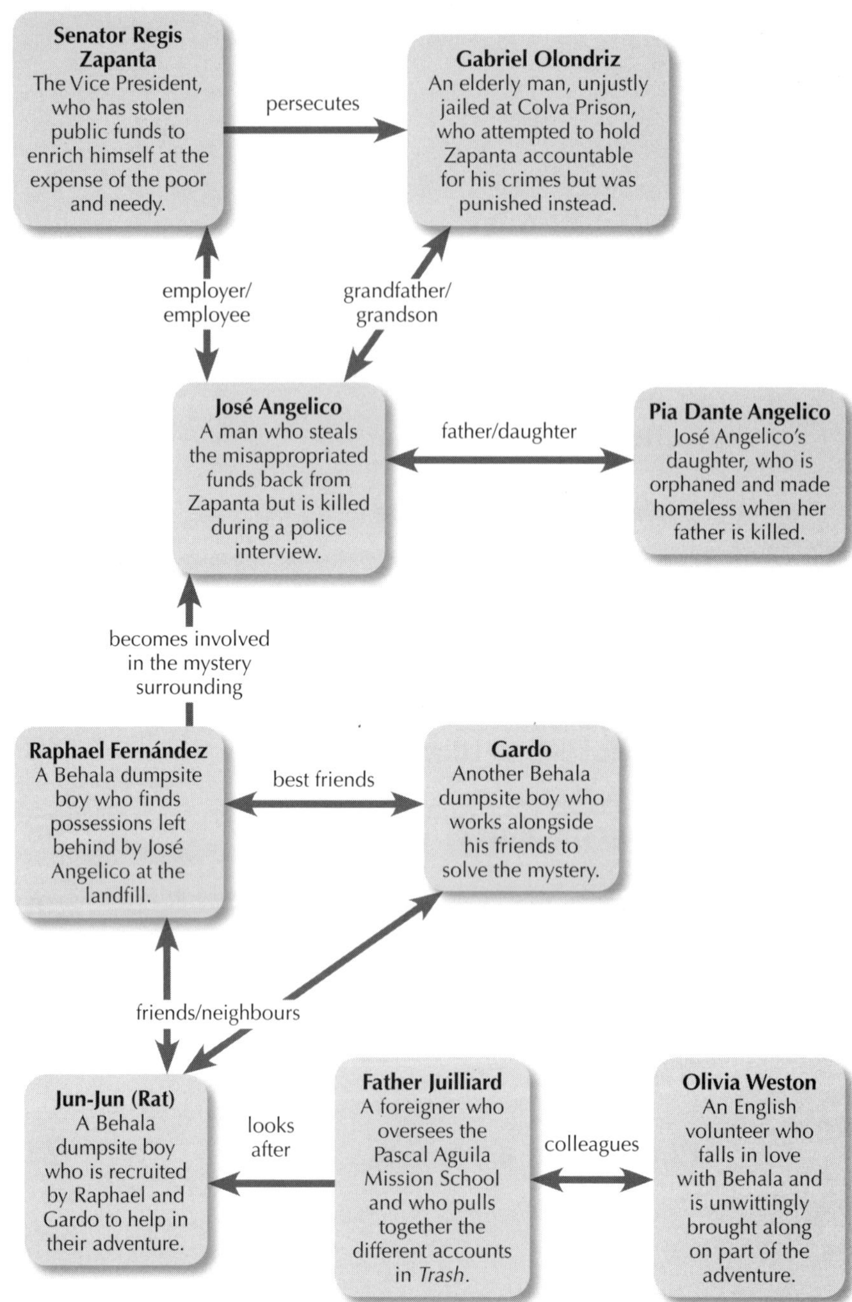

OVERVIEW

About the author

Andy Mulligan is an English-born writer who began his career as a theatre director. After travelling through Asia as a young man and seeing countless children in need, he decided to retrain as a teacher. On receiving his qualifications, he returned to Asia to teach English and Drama, working at schools in India, Vietnam and the Philippines, in addition to a stint in Brazil. These experiences helped to shape his world view and inspired him to begin writing.

His first novel, *Ribblestrop,* was published in 2009 and set at an unusual English boarding school. The school's motto is 'life is dangerous', and its eclectic bunch of students face a roofless mansion, underground tunnels and possible ghosts. He returned to these characters in the sequels *Return to Ribblestrop* in 2011 and *Ribblestrop Forever!* in 2012.

Mulligan published *Trash* in 2010. Drawing on his experiences working in the Philippines, he based the novel's fictional setting of Behala on a real dumpsite he visited in Manila. Extraordinarily, he wrote the entire novel in just ten days. The book brought him international acclaim, and he took a sabbatical from teaching to focus on writing.

Mulligan has won several literary prizes and his writing, including the young adult novels *The Boy With Two Heads, Liquidator* and *Dog,* has been translated into thirty-two languages. In 2014, *Trash* was adapted into a film directed by three-time Academy Award nominee Stephen Daldry. In 2019, Mulligan published his first adult novel, *Train Man.*

Synopsis

Set at an enormous rubbish dump, Behala, in an unnamed country, *Trash* is narrated by various characters whose testimonies, we are told, have been compiled by Father Juilliard, who runs the poorly attended Mission School. The residents of Behala live in ramshackle shanties among mountains of garbage. Rather than attend the school established for Behala children, many young people spend their days picking through the landfill to support their families. They rarely come across any items of particular value and are more accustomed to encountering human waste.

Yet one day, fourteen-year-old Raphael discovers a bag containing several unusual and perplexing items: a wallet, a considerable amount of cash, a key, a map, some photographs and an ID card. Raphael enlists his friends Gardo and Jun-Jun, better known as 'Rat', to help find the original owner of the bag, José Angelico, and piece together the puzzle of clues he left behind.

After locating the locker to which the key belongs, the boys find an envelope with a cryptic code and a letter from José to his grandfather Gabriel Olondriz. They work out that José died in police custody after being accused of stealing money from his employer, Vice President Senator Zapanta. Despite this, José's friends and colleagues reported that he was a good and kind man. The boys also learn that José left behind a young daughter, Pia Dante, and that Gabriel is currently serving a life sentence in prison.

Their investigation is interrupted by a raid on Behala by the police, who apprehend a terrified Raphael and drive him to a distant police station where he is interrogated, threatened and assaulted. At one point, Raphael is choked and dangled from a window, yet he refuses to yield, continuing to deny any knowledge of José's bag.

Raphael returns to Behala, and the boys trick Sister Olivia, a volunteer at the Mission School, into escorting Gardo to Colva Prison in order to speak to Gabriel. Although old and unwell, Gabriel confirms that he was imprisoned after accusing Senator Zapanta of corruption when millions of dollars earmarked for public services vanished. Gabriel was then arrested on trumped-up murder charges. He advises that the cryptic code found in the locker corresponds to a Bible he owns, but the visit is terminated by a prison guard before he can pass the book on.

Meanwhile, Raphael and Jun-Jun await Gardo's return. For their own safety, the two decide they cannot return to Behala. Knowing they need funds to continue their search, Jun-Jun reveals a stash of money he had been saving with the intention of returning to his homeland and working as a fisherman. The boys use Jun-Jun's money to rent a room to hide out in, before deciding to head to Zapanta's mansion in Green Hills.

Shocked by the opulence of Zapanta's home, Raphael and Jun-Jun befriend a gardener on the grounds of the mansion, who confirms that his boss has been stealing money for years and that José possibly smuggled Zapanta's stolen money out of his home via an old refrigerator.

After the three boys reunite, they rendezvous with the prison guard, who has Gabriel's Bible. When the guard demands an exorbitant bribe to hand over the Bible, Jun-Jun sneaks back to the Mission School to steal the money needed. After taking the money from Father Juilliard's safe, Jun-Jun feels guilty. Unable to read or write, he leaves behind a drawing for the priest in the hope that he will be forgiven.

When Gardo meets with the prison guard to hand over the money, he realises he is being set up by the police, so quickly snatches the Bible and slashes the guard's face with his rubbish hook. That night, the boys decode the cryptic note using the Bible and decipher a message: '*Go to the map ref where we lay look for the brightest light my child*' (p.157). Finding the map coordinates leads the boys to a graveyard. It is a hive of activity because of the Day of the Dead festival and is divided into wealthy and poor sides. The poor, tending to their families' graves by candlelight, form 'the brightest of lights' (p.180) and lead the boys to the graves of the Angelico family, including one engraved for Pia Dante. A little girl appears, revealing she is Pia, hungry and weak but very much alive. The boys realise that the money must be buried in the grave her father had purchased in her name. They crack open the grave and find the missing millions.

After returning the money stolen from Father Juilliard and scattering the remaining money throughout Behala, the boys, along with Pia, travel to Jun-Jun's homeland of Sampalo and fulfil his dream of fishing in his island paradise.

Character summaries

Raphael Fernández

A fourteen-year-old 'dumpsite boy' (p.3), Raphael's discovery of the mysterious bag among the trash is the catalyst for the mystery at the centre of the story. Raphael lives with his aunt and cousins at Behala, a massive garbage dump where he rummages through waste to find items worth selling. Strong, resilient and compassionate, despite his young age, he is able to outwit and outsmart adults at every turn.

Gardo

Also fourteen, Raphael's best friend works alongside him at the Behala landfill. More serious and solemn than Raphael, the boys are nonetheless close and remain united against overwhelming odds. Like Raphael, Gardo displays courage and determination that belies his young age.

Jun-Jun (Rat)

Also known as 'Rat' because he lives alone with only rats for company, Jun-Jun is slightly younger than the other two boys. He is also malnourished and filthy, which allows him to blend in with the other poor children and sneak around without being detected. Streetwise, wily and shrewd, his contributions to solving the mystery are vital. He gradually learns to trust the others, and the three boys eventually form their own makeshift family unit.

Father Juilliard

The sixty-three-year-old foreigner oversees the Pascal Aguila Mission School but struggles with feelings of futility over whether his contributions are of any consequence. Inadvertently manipulated by the boys in their quest, he nevertheless harbours no ill feelings towards them. On the contrary, Father Juilliard reveals a fondness and even admiration for how the boys survive, even when they resort to dishonest tactics.

Olivia Weston

Referred to as 'Sister' by the boys, Olivia is a young English volunteer who has fallen in love with Behala. Sensitive and kind, she curses her own naivety and gullibility in getting involved in the boys' scheming. Even so, she remains grateful for having her eyes opened to the harsher realities of the world.

Senator Regis Zapanta

The corrupt Vice President who stole and embezzled public funds to enrich himself, Zapanta uses his position of authority to stamp out dissent, threatening and even ordering the killing of his adversaries.

José Angelico

A deceased houseboy to Senator Zapanta, José devises a plan to steal back the funds his employer misappropriated in order to redistribute them to the poor. Before being killed for his efforts, he left behind letters and a series of clues that Raphael, Gardo and Jun-Jun ultimately decipher to accomplish his goals.

Gabriel Olondriz

José's grandfather is an elderly prisoner on the verge of death. Unjustly jailed when he attempted to draw attention to the crimes of Senator Zapanta, he assists Gardo with unravelling the mystery before he dies.

Pia Dante Angelico

The orphaned eight-year-old daughter of José. She is taken under the wing of Raphael, Gardo and Jun-Jun, who fulfil her father's dying wish that she be rescued and taken care of.

BACKGROUND & CONTEXT

Although *Trash* is set in an unnamed country, references to several real Manila landmarks suggest that the novel takes place in the island country of the Philippines. The Manila locations referred to include Buendia, McKinley, Green Hills and Fort Barton, while Jun-Jun's homeland of Sampalo is potentially a reference to the district of Sampaloc.

Located in the Pacific Ocean, the Philippines is an archipelago consisting of thousands of islands divided into three main regions: Luzon, Visayas and Mindanao. According to the United Nations, the Philippines is considered a lower-middle-income country with an emerging economy. A population of approximately 114 million people makes the Philippines the twelfth most populated country in the world. Manila, its capital, is home to nearly two million people, making it the most densely populated city in the world. As such, Manila faces overcrowding, housing shortages, pollution, sanitation issues, traffic congestion and a widening chasm between the rich and the poor.

These issues often overshadow what is a breathtakingly beautiful country, adorned with mountains, forests, rivers and extensive coastlines. Although the country's industries are growing, the region's economy predominantly relies on agriculture. The nation's currency is the Philippine peso, subdivided into 100 sentimo (or centavos).

Reflecting the setting's tropical climate, Mulligan's characters refer to the inevitability of monsoons throughout the novel. The Philippines is also susceptible to monsoons, as well as to volcanic eruptions, tsunamis and earthquakes, because of its proximity to the tectonic belt known as the Pacific Ring of Fire.

One less-than-scenic Manila location referred to in the novel is Smokey (or Smoky) Mountain, a dumpsite that operated in the city for half a century. Tens of thousands of Filipinos lived in and around the dumpsite, building homes in slums nearby and making their living by scouring the waste.

In *Trash*, Mulligan refers to a tragedy that occurred at the site, which parallels a landslide that occurred at Smokey Mountain's successor, Payatas, another massive dumpsite in Manila established in the 1970s and officially closed in 2017. In July 2000, hundreds of Payatas dumpsite residents were crushed to death or burned alive when piles of garbage collapsed on top of their makeshift homes. This tragic loss of life highlights the vulnerability of dumpsite workers and residents who risk everything to make a living.

While Mulligan's Behala is fictional, it shares many similarities with Payatas and two additional Manila dumpsites at *Barangay* (meaning village) Aroma and Angono. At these sites, thousands of scavengers work through the tonnes of waste produced daily. In recent years, the workers at the largest dumpsite, Payatas, have taken the initiative to improve their conditions, organising themselves into the Payatas Alliance Recycling Exchange to run the site more efficiently. Food waste is sold to farmers for their livestock, biogas released by the waste is turned into electricity and anything of value is sold at nearby junk shops, including plastic, aluminium and scrap metal.

Yet these stories of efficiency, symbiosis and a commitment to environmental sustainability mask a darker and more disturbing reality of poverty and inequality. In countless developing countries, cast-offs and waste from wealthier residents are picked over by the poor and uneducated, who have few or no other ways to make a living. Among the millions of people existing in this manner are countless children who are forced to forgo education just to survive. Despite human rights charters and labour laws designed to protect children, there seems to be no end in sight to this problem, with experts suggesting that household waste will double over the coming decades. These child waste-pickers, along with their adult counterparts, face unsanitary, hazardous and potentially deadly conditions each day.

The Philippines is certainly not alone when it comes to impoverished children forced to seek employment rather than education. Some researchers estimate that one in six children in the world is engaged in some sort of labour. Like the children in Mulligan's novel, many of them work in difficult and dangerous situations, putting their health and safety at risk to provide for themselves and their families.

Several charities and non-government organisation (NGO) initiatives have been established in Manila in an attempt to improve the lives of those living and working at the dumpsites. Many of these operations are religious, like the Pascal Aguila Mission School in the novel. Christian missions date back hundreds of years; they provide aid, clothing, food and medicine to those in need, but often, help is supplied with caveats and conditions. Many charities have been criticised for taking advantage of impoverished people, their philanthropy a cover for their real mission of evangelism and religious conversion.

The Philippines experienced significant political turmoil in the twentieth century, which impacts how many citizens view the government. The most infamous leader in recent decades is President Ferdinand Marcos, a dictator who led the country from 1965 until 1986. After being fairly and democratically elected, Marcos seized control of the military and refused to step down when his initial term was over. He suspended the parliament, rigged elections, jailed his opposition and declared martial law. In this time, it is estimated that he stole billions of dollars of public funds. While the majority of Filipinos lived on approximately a dollar a day, the Marcos family lived in luxury, despite a presidential salary of only around $10 000 a year. A non-violent revolution known as the People Power Revolution overthrew President Marcos, who fled to the United States with his family and died in 1989. Marcos was never held accountable for the missing funds nor for the numerous human rights violations and other crimes he committed as leader.

The country is now proudly democratic and, ironically, led by Ferdinand Marcos' son, Bongbong Marcos. In recent years the government has made some strides in eliminating corruption. By 2023, the Philippines was rated the 115th least corrupt nation out of the 180 countries measured by the Corruption Perceptions Index.

Despite the challenges of poverty and inequality, the Philippines is home to a rich, diverse and ancient culture. Roman Catholicism is the dominant religion, with Protestants and Muslims making up a sizeable minority. Although part of Southeast Asia, the region is heavily influenced by the West because it was colonised by the Spanish. In fact, the country gets its name from King Philip II, the sixteenth-century monarch who oversaw the expansion of the Spanish Empire and the occupation of the area. Since the colonial period, Catholicism has been a fundamental part of the identities of millions of Filipinos. The Church's close associations with the culture of much of the country has placed it at the centre of nationalist and social justice movements (Harvard Divinity School 2024).

One cultural observance that plays a prominent role in the narrative of *Trash* is the Day of the Dead, which incorporates All Saints' Day and All Souls' Day and is sometimes referred to as Undas, Araw ng mga Patay or Todos los Santos. During this celebration, those who celebrate traditionally pay tribute to their deceased relatives by praying, cleaning and repairing graves and tombstones, and providing offerings of flowers, candles and food.

Mulligan's choice to avoid referring to the Philippines or Manila by name in the book is his subtle way of reminding readers that this story could be set in any number of places around the world. Mulligan was also hesitant to identify the country lest his writing be seen as a criticism of any particular place. In fact, when *Trash* was adapted into a film in 2014, the setting was seamlessly shifted to Brazil, with the children speaking Portuguese.

GENRE, STRUCTURE & LANGUAGE

Genre

Young adult novels are often referred to as coming-of-age texts or bildungsromans, a German term derived from the words for 'education' and 'novel'. Essentially, these tales focus on protagonists learning and growing as they develop from children into adults. These characters are confronted with the harsh realities of adult life and learn about the world and their place in it. This often involves a loss of innocence, the idealistic cocoon of childhood being left behind as they overcome obstacles and learn to persevere despite life's challenges.

In writing *Trash*, Mulligan was inspired by two very different stories about young people: John Boyne's *The Boy in the Striped Pyjamas* and Roald Dahl's *Charlie and the Chocolate Factory*. The former is a historical novel about a young boy growing up in Nazi Germany. Mulligan aimed to produce an equally compelling story about a young person who, like Boyne's protagonist, is confronted with an ugly adult world of corruption, brutality and inhumanity. The latter is a more light-hearted novel about a poor young boy who is given an opportunity to better himself and his family when he finds a lucky 'golden ticket'.

Trash is a realist novel set in a recognisable world, and fits relatively neatly within this young adult genre. However, Mulligan's novel might also be classified as a thriller – a story infused with elements of mystery and suspense. Stories in this genre are often crime-related, with the protagonists (along with the reader) needing to solve a puzzle to resolve the suspense. Such narratives are often laced with clues, plot twists and cliffhangers to engage and thrill readers.

As a crime is often at the centre of such stories, many focus on a protagonist who is either a detective, a private investigator or an amateur sleuth who feels compelled to crack a case. Authors Arthur Conan Doyle, Agatha Christie and Raymond Chandler made household names of their heroes, Sherlock Holmes, Hercule Poirot and Philip Marlowe, who all used their wits to investigate and solve numerous mysteries.

In the twentieth century, stories of young amateur sleuths became immensely popular. Edward Stratemeyer's *Nancy Drew* and *The Hardy Boys*, and Edith Blyton's *The Famous Five* and *The Secret Seven*, all featured the adventures of young people encountering stolen treasures, drug smugglers, bank robbers and possible ghosts. The young protagonists are forced to take matters into their own hands when the adults are either absent, oblivious or too corrupt to be trusted. The young people often bond through working together to unpack clues, overcome numerous obstacles and, ultimately, solve the mystery. Mulligan's Raphael, Gardo and Jun-Jun, like the child sleuths before them, are certainly motivated by a sense of justice and demonstrate an admirable moral core, yet they are also caught up in a thrilling adventure.

Structure

Although in many ways a conventional young adult mystery with a linear narration, Mulligan's novel is deceptively complex. The story unravels over five parts, changes first-person narrators frequently and even switches text types from traditional narration to newspapers and letters.

When switching point of view, the narrators often explain why another character is in a better position to tell the story, happily passing the baton in a relay of storytelling. The characters admit to lacking the whole picture and invite their friends, colleagues and acquaintances to help recount events. Gardo hints at the idea of an unreliable narrator and the limitations of a subjective point of view, telling the reader that 'we agreed to split the story because some things [Raphael] forgets' (p.27). At times, Mulligan shifts to a minor character's perspective for a single chapter and never visits this perspective again.

The various threads of the narrative overlap, with different stories sometimes occuring concurrently. For example, the chapters about Gardo visiting the prison with Olivia are interspersed with Raphael and Jun-Jun's adventures while they wait for their friend.

Throughout the chronological narration, Mulligan uses foreshadowing to signpost upcoming events. This includes explicit teasers for the reader, such as 'we were in something deep, getting deeper' (p.43) and 'things were about to get very dangerous' (p.84).

Although the narration is fragmented by design, the story moves at a rollicking pace, benefitting from the deft hand of Father Juilliard, who tells the reader 'I am the one pulling these accounts together' (p.47). This suggests that he is the editor and eventual publisher of the story, assembling it after the events have occurred and helping the reader to make sense of its complexities.

Language

Mulligan's characters address the reader directly in a conversational manner, each with their own distinct voice. The boys begin their storytelling with a sense of wonder, all somewhat naive, but eventually develop greater confidence and resilience. Despite confronting subject matter including corruption, violence and death, much of the narration is imbued with the boys' humour, which often involves the use of sarcasm and mockery to make light of a disturbing situation.

The language choices of the adult characters, Father Juilliard, Olivia Weston, Frederico Gonz and Grace, in addition to the letter from José Angelico, serve as a stark contrast to the idealism and wonderment of the younger characters. As the boys gradually discover the dark underbelly of society, the adult narrators reveal a sense of world-weariness and a resignation to the evils in the world.

The characters are all honest and reflective in their storytelling. Often, these testimonies and recollections feel as though they are speaking in a confessional, as the characters wrestle with their choices and their sense of guilt.

Although written in a conversational style, Mulligan occasionally employs sensory language and imagery to immerse readers into this distinct world. The sights, sounds and even smells of Behala and the surrounding areas are carefully and skilfully rendered, from 'the valleys ... the mountains ... the docks to the marshes, one whole long world of steaming trash' at Behala (p.4) to the 'thin bodies, glistening with sweat ... and a smell of old food, sweat and urine' of Colva Prison (p.94). To further locate readers in this unique setting, Filipino colloquialisms and cultural references are scattered throughout the narration.

Symbolism

As tension mounts over the course of the story, the weather often reflects a sense of uncertainty and anticipation. There are several references to the inevitability of a drastic change in weather. The boys hear 'talk of a freak typhoon coming in from the sea' and sense 'real heat in the breeze' (p.86). The tropical storm threatens to up-end their world, just as the boys' detective work threatens to topple their corrupt leaders.

These weather references often parallel new twists and turns in the narrative, with Jun-Jun stating that 'we knew this was real, scary heat ... we all felt something big was coming' (p.141). Although the boys seem accustomed to such tropical weather quirks, this storm is ominously referred to as a 'freak typhoon' (e.g. p.86 and p.177), symbolising the new, chaotic and dangerous world they now find themselves in.

The literal typhoon never eventuates, with the final reference to weather occurring in the denouement of the story as the boys harness the city's stirring winds to distribute the stolen funds around Behala. In this final goodbye gesture, 'the notes spilled out and whirled ... a hurricane of money' (p.199). Instead of signifying danger, the typhoon winds ironically facilitate an act of altruism.

Several religious references also appear throughout the story. The Bible plays a vital role in the plot, one of Raphael's few possessions is 'a cup with a picture of the Virgin Mary' (p.17), and many of the characters have names with religious connotations. José Angelico is sacrificed as a Christ-like martyr and the final mystery is revealed on All Souls' Day at a Catholic graveyard, where Jun-Jun declares, 'I had never been watched over by so many saints' (p.178). The novel suggests that religion provides the boys with a strong moral core and something to turn to in difficult times. Raphael mentions 'saying a prayer' (p.8) and tells the reader, 'I prayed in my head' (p.67), and at one point, Olivia notices that Gardo's lips moved 'as if he was saying a prayer' (p.87). At one of tensest junctures of the story, Gardo describes 'praying to God that both [his] friends were safe' (p.152). Jun-Jun compares Senator Zapanta's mansion to 'the promised land', stating, 'I felt like little Moses' (p.120). The diminutive sizes of the three boys contrast with those of the older, larger and stronger adults they find themselves up against, in what might be read as an allusion to the Biblical story of David and Goliath's battle in which a boy outwits and defeats a giant.

The references to religious practices and iconography remind readers of the rich culture of the characters, in addition to highlighting the innate goodness of the protagonists. The boys' actions reflect many of the core tenets of Christianity, particularly that of altruism. Their final act of distributing millions of dollars to the impoverished residents of Behala parallels that of Jesus feeding the needy with loaves and fishes. Gabriel Olondriz recognises the virtuousness of the boys, calling Gardo 'a young, sainted angel' (p.131).

The morality of the boys is accentuated through the motif of light among the dark. When interrogated and assaulted by the police, Raphael notices that the area he has been taken to has 'no lights', lamenting that he has 'never felt so lost and lonely' (p.57). The many references to different types of light throughout the story, from candlelight and headlights to floodlights and flashlights, remind readers of the potential for goodness when all seems lost. 'The brightest of lights' (p.180) the boys seek turns out to be within: a core sense of morality and goodness, represented by brightness in a world of darkness and treasures that lurk among the trash.

CHAPTER-BY-CHAPTER ANALYSIS

PART ONE – Chapter 1 (pp.3–6)

Summary: *Raphael narrates. He introduces the reader to Behala.*

The first chapter orients the reader and introduces them to the first of the novel's several narrators. Raphael Fernández is a fourteen-year-old boy who lives and works at a massive garbage dump, Behala, scouring the discarded rubbish for items of worth. The landfill is 'about two hundred football pitches big, or maybe a thousand basketball courts' and emits a stench so pungent 'you can smell Behala long before you see it' (p.4).

Although Raphael is certainly impoverished, living in a shanty house with his aunt and cousins, there is not an ounce of self-pity about him. Selfless and resourceful, Raphael seems mostly resigned to his lot in life. He cheerfully refers to himself as a 'dumpsite boy' (p.3) and retains a healthy sense of wonder and humour about his situation.

Raphael has been working at Behala for eleven years, giving up on attending the local Mission School to help provide for his family. While Raphael and his friend Gardo use hooks to fossick for any items of value to sell, repurpose or reuse, they often find themselves among human excrement, or '*stuppa*' (p.1). Raphael initially dismisses the notion that 'interesting things' (p.4) are waiting to be unearthed or that 'something nice' (p.5) could emerge from trash. Yet he teases the reader by stating that one day, something valuable *was* discovered.

Key vocabulary

Stuppa/Stupp: a colloquial term for human waste.

Mission: a religious establishment or organisation that provides services to the less fortunate.

PART ONE – Chapter 2 (pp.7–9)

Summary: *Raphael narrates. A small leather bag is found among the trash, piquing Raphael's interest.*

Raphael is working alongside Gardo underneath giant cranes and conveyer belts, a strategic position that ensures they get first dibs on the newest, untouched trash. Among the garbage he finds a small leather bag containing a map, a wallet, eleven hundred pesos, an ID card belonging to a man called José Angelico, two photos of a young girl and a key with a yellow tag with the number 101. Although a windfall, Raphael's narration hints that such a find turns out to be somewhat of a mixed blessing, describing the day he found it as 'my unlucky-lucky day, the day the world turned upside down' (p.7).

Although Raphael's first instinct is to try to return the possessions to José Angelico, he realises the futility of trying to find him in such a large city. He is quite taken by the photographs of José and the young girl, both of whom appear sad, he with 'frightened eyes' and she with a 'serious face … as if no one had told her to smile' (p.9), foreshadowing the serious and tragic story that will unfold. As the chapter concludes, Raphael is now in possession of José's key and he says, with metaphorical intent, '*Everyone needs a key*. With the right key, you can bust the door wide open. Because nobody's going to open it for you' (p.9). The door to Raphael's new world has indeed swung open.

PART ONE – Chapter 3 (pp.10–18)

Summary: *Raphael narrates. The police come looking for José Angelico's bag. Distrusting them, Raphael pretends he hasn't found it.*

The police arrive at Behala, a rare occurrence given there's little crime in the area; as Raphael explains, 'There's not a lot to steal, and we don't usually steal from each other' (p.10). The police offer a reward for the missing bag, and Raphael weighs up whether to accept it, wondering if they would actually pay up. He decides he needs time to think.

The police say the missing bag is linked to a crime. Although Raphael's aunt reveals that her nephew indeed found something, Raphael quickly lies and says all he found was a shoe. The presence of the police confirms to Raphael that there must be more to the story of the bag. At this point, Raphael has a slight crisis of conscience, uneasy about deceiving his aunt and worried that 'things were going to get complicated' (p.16).

Gardo insists they must move the bag to a safer location. They decide to enlist the help of a young boy they call Rat, because he lives in 'the only place they're not gonna look' (p.17).

PART ONE – Chapter 4 (pp.19–26)

Summary: *Raphael narrates. Jun-Jun agrees to help Raphael and Gardo.*

Raphael and Gardo light candles to guide them to Rat's abode. Rat, whose real name is Jun-Jun, is younger than the other two and lives among the rats in a hole under piles of garbage. Even at a dumpsite like Behala, we learn there is a hierarchy, and Jun-Jun is at the bottom of the social order, being skinny, illiterate and with only vermin for company. Raphael pityingly observes that 'a lot of kids would just throw things at him and laugh' (p.23).

The other two boys ask Jun-Jun to hide José Angelico's bag, and say they'll pay him for the favour. Jun-Jun agrees, and they show him its contents. Noticing the key among José's possessions, Jun-Jun tells the boys that it comes from a locker at Central Station. He recognises the key, having once lived at the train station, and offers to take them there. The author has now created a central group of three boys as the story's protagonists.

PART ONE – Chapter 5 (pp.27–35)

Summary: *Gardo narrates. The boys' sense of guilt and worry escalates.*

Gardo takes over the narration from Raphael, explaining that 'some things [Raphael] forgets' (p.27). Raphael is anxious to head to Central Station immediately, but Gardo reminds him of the danger they are both in. They decide it is best to keep up appearances by pretending to search for the missing bag, waiting another day before heading to the station.

Although the two boys are as close as brothers, we are realising the differences in their motivations, temperaments and maturity levels. Where Raphael is excitable and impulsive, Gardo is cautious and more sensible. While scrounging around the dumpsite with the rest of Behala, Gardo worries that their refusal to cooperate with the police might prevent a killer from being caught.

Later, Auntie confronts the two boys about sneaking out at night and wants reassurance that the family is not in any danger. Raphael promises that they are safe, although he and Gardo are afraid. Gardo admits that he 'couldn't meet her eye' (p.34).

Raphael and Gardo stay up all night, strategising and plotting their next move. Ominously, Gardo confides to the reader that they were overconfident in thinking they could evade the police.

PART ONE – Chapter 6 (pp.36–43)

Summary: *Raphael narrates. The boys head to Central Station and find more clues.*

The three boys head to Central Station, but must negotiate with the 'station boys' (p.38) who protect their territory from outsiders. Jun-Jun uses his street smarts and quick wits to avoid the police, guards and crowds of people, bribing the station boys and clearing the way to José Angelico's locker.

Inside they find a package containing a letter addressed to a prisoner called Gabriel Olondriz, in addition to a slip of paper containing a mysterious code. They are left with even more questions, and a series of clues to somehow untangle. Raphael concludes this section by admitting that 'all we were sure of was that we were in something deep, getting deeper' (p.43).

Q What qualities or attributes do Raphael, Gardo and Jun-Jun already possess that will help them on their journey?

Q Why do Raphael and Gardo feel compelled to lie to both the police and Raphael's aunt?

Q The protagonists have already hinted that things are about to get worse. What is the threat? What danger might they be in?

PART TWO – Chapter 1 (pp.47–54)

Summary: *Father Juilliard narrates. He is a religious father by profession and a father figure at heart.*

This chapter introduces Father Juilliard and we learn of the challenges he faces running the Pascal Aguila Mission School. The school struggles to get students to attend, has financial issues and is stiflingly hot. Father Juilliard suggests that his involvement in this story means he is being forced to retire and may even need to leave the country.

Despite his position of authority, Father Juilliard boldly states, 'I have always said that you have to break the rules. I set rules up; then I break them' (p.48), demonstrating a rebellious streak that challenges the stereotype of a devout man. He also describes Pascal Aguila, whom his school is named after, and we learn that the school and its students honour a man who 'fought corruption and was shot to death for his pains' (p.49). The author is describing two more instances of people rebelling against authority to do what is right – Father Juilliard and Pascal Aguila. After Father Juilliard describes Aguila's murder, he says, 'in this country, the dead are very important' (p.50), foreshadowing the importance of both the dead man José Angelico and the Day of the Dead.

Before the events of this story, Father Juilliard had only passing familiarity with Raphael and Gardo, but was well acquainted with Jun-Jun, whom he supported with food and medicine. The boys approach Father Juilliard with a request to use his computer, telling him a concocted cover story about entering a quiz. Father Juilliard shows genuine fondness for and compassion towards the boys, and feels frustrated that there are so many children living in poverty: 'it breaks your heart' (p.53). He even questions whether education is of any value to those more focused on survival, bemoaning, 'it's easy to think what you do in a school like this is of absolutely no consequence or good to anyone' (p.53).

Key vocabulary

Po: a colloquial word used to show respect to elders; used by Jun-Jun in his conversations with Father Juilliard.

PART TWO – Chapter 2 (pp.55–67)

Summary: *Raphael narrates. The police apprehend Raphael and violently interrogate him, yet he remains stoic and steadfast.*

This chapter warns readers, 'now it gets serious' (p.55), with Raphael noting that 'this is going to be very difficult to write about' (p.56). Four vans of police officers arrive to search Raphael's home and, upon finding nothing, promptly arrest him. Despite the protestations of Gardo, Auntie and many of his neighbours, Raphael is dragged into a police van and whisked away.

Raphael is sick from fear, unable to stop crying as he is driven to a more deserted area that houses a police station. His pitiful declaration that he has 'never felt so lost and lonely' (p.57) does not stop him from remaining stubbornly resolute; he decides that whatever threats or consequences he might face, he won't cooperate, having already come so far and learned so much.

Not only are the police menacing, but they are patronising too, surprised that Raphael can read, threatening his loved ones and mocking them by referring to them as 'your stinking little family' (p.64). The fact that Raphael is a child does not prevent the authorities from resorting to violence. Raphael is forcefully struck, ending up on the floor. He can taste blood in his mouth, and he has soiled himself out of fear. Yet he remains resolute, so one of the police officers holds him by the ankles and dangles him out of a window. The police force, ironically an organisation designed to serve and protect citizens, seems to be yet another cog in a wheel of widespread corruption.

Despite this David-and-Goliath-style clash, Raphael courageously refuses to break, reminding himself of the promise he made to Gardo and Jun-Jun not to tell. Surprised at his own strength, he attributes it to the memory of José Angelico. When eventually released, he finds himself running fast, reflecting, 'At least I was free, and at least – unlike poor José Angelico – I was alive … I knew then that I could run for ever' (p.67). Despite his youth, Raphael survives the type of interrogation that tragically José did not.

PART TWO – Chapter 3 (pp.68–71)

Summary: *Raphael narrates. The truth about José Angelico begins to emerge.*

The weather has changed. The rain has brought coolness and typhoon breezes blow despite this being the dry season.

Key point

Mulligan has opted for a change of weather here. Consider the symbolic meaning of this, and what it suggests about what has changed or shifted in the story.

Raphael continues running, feeling lucky to have escaped death. He is proud that a garbage boy has outwitted the police. Looking at a statue of a soldier, he sees parallels between the soldier's battles and his, and is inspired to keep fighting.

At this point, Raphael reveals the information he found on Father Juilliard's computer. While Raphael was initially concerned that José Angelico could have been a murderer, it turns out he was a victim instead. He had died at a police station, paralleling Raphael's own near-death experience. After leaving Father Juilliard's office Raphael had managed to find some old newspapers that covered the incident, learning that José had been arrested for stealing six million dollars from his employer, Senator Zapanta. Raphael had also found out that José was an orphan who had been adopted by Gabriel Olondriz' son, and that he had a young daughter, which makes Raphael even more determined to deliver the letter to Gabriel at Colva Prison.

PART TWO – Chapter 4 (pp.72–3)

Summary: *Grace narrates. She tempers the lies about José with her first-hand knowledge of him.*

This brief chapter is the only one narrated by Senator Zapanta's maid Grace, who has been asked by Father Juilliard to share her recollections of José Angelico. This chapter serves to correct the media narrative of José as a thief, as Grace instead remembers him as 'kind, gentle, trustworthy and honest' (p.72).

The two worked together as domestic servants for Zapanta. Grace knew that José had lost both his wife and young son, but had a daughter, Pia Dante. Grace says José paid for Pia to board with a family so that she could attend school. After hearing of José's death, Grace attempted to locate Pia, but she had gone, lost among the many street children. Grace vows never to forget José, whom she calls 'a good man' (p.73). Despite his physical absence in the narrative, his shadow and legacy loom large.

Q What is the impact of switching narrators? How do the adults see things differently from the boys?

Q Why is Father Juilliard so conflicted about his job and his role at Behala?

Q How does Raphael remain strong and determined despite being severely threatened? What motivates him at this point?

PART THREE – Chapter 1 (pp.77–83)

Summary: *Olivia narrates. The 'house-mother' is unwittingly caught up in the boys' plans.*

This chapter is narrated by Olivia Weston, a young British woman who is travelling the world. Intending to briefly visit the dumpsite to deliver some sponsorship money, Olivia's plans were uprooted when she saw Behala, and she decided to stay, explaining, 'Behala had hit me hard, and I couldn't get it out of my mind' (p.77). She compares this to falling in love, declaring that Behala has changed her life. In her time there, Olivia has contributed via teaching, feeding the children, administering first aid and working on a water-sanitation project. Although only twenty-two, she fills a maternal role as a 'temporary house-mother' (p.77).

Olivia is approached by the boys for assistance. Noticing the bruises on Raphael, she shows she is sensitive and empathetic but braces herself to deny any requests for money. She's surprised when, instead of begging for cash, they request she accompany them to a prison. They tell her that Gardo's grandfather has been wrongly imprisoned, and they urgently need to speak to him, believing they will be able to gain access to the prison with Olivia as she is a foreigner and a social worker. Despite some initial reservations and protestations, Olivia reluctantly agrees, later cursing her 'vanity and stupidity' (p.82), which she sees as the reason for her believing their deception. Yet again, the boys are outwitting the adults in their world, a testament to their charms and survival instincts.

Olivia escorts Gardo to the prison, first stopping to buy him new clothes, commenting on how a simple makeover transforms the boy: 'He emerged from the changing room, and he was simply no longer a Behala dumpsite boy! He was taller, he was bursting with confidence and smiles' (p.83).

PART THREE – Chapter 2 (p.84)

Summary: *Father Juilliard narrates. He reckons with feelings of guilt and complicity.*

Father Juilliard interjects with a one-page chapter, chastising himself for getting Olivia mixed up in the boys' adventures and not intervening. Despite his many years of experience at Behala, he keeps being manipulated and having his trust broken, as the boys 'are the best liars in the world' (p.84). More foreshadowing occurs here when Father Juilliard indicates that the worst is yet to come: 'Things were about to get very dangerous indeed' (p.84).

PART THREE – Chapter 3 (pp.85–92)

Summary: *Olivia narrates. She and Gardo enter Colva Prison.*

As Olivia describes travelling to Colva Prison, she admits that, in retrospect, she knows 'it was stupid' (p.85). When driving through Colva, she's struck by how much more impoverished the area is than Behala. The prisoners' families live close to the jail so they can provide their loved ones with food – if they don't, the prisoners are left to starve, revealing yet another layer of the unjust social hierarchy in which the poor are forgotten and left to fend for themselves.

Gardo tenderly holds Olivia's hand as they approach the prison, each as fearful as the other. She ponders what will happen if she enters the prison and is not let out again. She realises that the line between freedom and incarceration is a fine one and that, despite her privileges, she is in a dangerous situation. Upon entering the prison, they are met by Mr Oliva, a social welfare officer who seems polite and friendly. Olivia and Mr Oliva seem to connect over their shared names and similar jobs, and he flatters her by telling her, 'Without people coming to help ... things would be worse than they are' (p.89).

Key point

Mulligan gives these unrelated characters similar names, which is an interesting choice. Initially, it highlights the parallels and similarities between them, both social workers among the poorer classes. Yet, as this part evolves, we see the stark contrasts between Olivia and Mr Oliva.

Mr Oliva questions whether it is Gabriel Olondriz they wish to visit, as the prisoner number they provided does not match theirs. He also reminds them that the prisoner is very sick and asks them to consider visiting another time. When Olivia insists the matter is urgent, Mr Oliva advises her that she will need to pay ten thousand pesos to fast-track her request. Olivia hands over the cash, understanding that in this city corruption is rampant and money talks.

Olivia and Gardo are led towards the prison. Listening to the animalistic shouts and laughter, the sounds of banging and doors slamming shut, Olivia compares her entrance into the prison to a descent into hell.

PART THREE – Chapter 4 (pp.93–6)

Summary: *Olivia narrates. Her heart bleeds for the prisoners and their oppressive conditions.*

Olivia describes feeling overwhelmed by the sight of prison cells so cramped that the prisoners are unable to stand up straight. Like the 'houses' in Behala, the cages are stacked on top of one another.

The prisoners cry out for assistance, but Olivia is powerless to help. She is stifled by the oppressive heat and overpowering smells. Yet rather than feel terrified or threatened, she is moved by the men's situation and cries pitiful tears for them. Despite their conditions, the prisoners are polite and considerate, calling Olivia 'ma'am'. Holding on to Gardo for support, she manages to work her way through the prison and into the hospital, feeling as though she might pass out.

When she expresses surprise to see children imprisoned, asking what they could possibly have done to deserve punishment, Gardo replies matter-of-factly that they are simply poor, a tragic indictment of an unjust society that the children have sadly become accustomed to.

An old man is brought to see them, his walking laboured even with the use of a stick. Olivia notices his 'burning white eyes' (p.96) and feels as though the old man has been waiting for her.

PART THREE – Chapter 5 (pp.97–102)

Summary: *Olivia narrates. Gabriel Olondriz reveals how he came to be imprisoned.*

Gabriel Olondriz is friendly and polite, grateful to receive visitors and happy to assist in any way he can. Olivia soon realises that the man is no relation to Gardo, yet despite her anger at being manipulated, she is more concerned with the prisoner's health. As Gabriel mops perspiration from his forehead, Olivia instinctively knows his condition is serious: 'The man was not simply weak: he was dying … I was certain of it' (p.98). Although Gardo is silent and still for much of the visit, he gently lifts a cup of water to the old man's lips, demonstrating tenderness.

Gabriel finally explains who he is and how he came to be imprisoned, highlighting the true extent of Senator Zapanta's deception and criminality. Thirty-five years previously, when serving as a 'small officer' (p.102), Gabriel brought corruption charges against Zapanta, the country's Vice President. Gabriel had sourced information that incriminated Zapanta in embezzling thirty million dollars of international aid money. The money had been earmarked for hospitals and schools, and should have been added to by the government and other organisations in a process called seed corning. Since the crime, the city has remained entrenched in poverty while the senator cruelly and selfishly benefitted.

However, the charges were never taken to court, and instead Gabriel found himself counter-sued and charged by powerful friends of Zapanta, highlighting the reach and resources of those in power. Gabriel ends his story with an ironic comment that soon his sentence will be over, his own death imminent.

Key vocabulary

Seed corn: an economic term meaning that a government will match a proportion of charitable funds or donations dollar for dollar (José Angelico also uses the term ironically in his letter to his grandfather on page 130).

PART THREE – Chapter 6 (p.103)

Summary: *Gardo narrates and conveys his regrets.*

Gardo takes over the narration to briefly apologise to Olivia for the deception that brought her to Colva Prison. He regrets not being able to tell her the entire truth, and explains that the boys had vowed to only trust one another. Selflessly, Gardo knew the danger they were facing and did not want her to know any more than was necessary, for her own safety. Gardo ends this brief chapter by asking Olivia for forgiveness.

PART THREE – Chapter 7 (pp.104–7)

Summary: *Olivia narrates. The truth about Gabriel's family causes agonising pain.*

The conversation with Gabriel continues via Olivia's narration as the old man outlines precisely how Zapanta managed to steal so many millions. Through creative accounting over time, the elected official was able to siphon a substantial amount of money, undoubtedly supported by others who 'probably thought they were doing our country a service' (p.104). Zapanta's crimes also seem to encompass murder, as a mysterious fire at Gabriel's home resulted in the deaths of two of his employees. Gabriel rues his naivety in thinking he would never be convicted on the fabricated charges, telling Olivia, 'I was stupid. In this country you pay for being stupid, just as you pay for being poor' (p.105).

Gardo interjects to explain he is in possession of an unsent letter from José Angelico. When Gardo confirms that Gabriel's grandson was killed by the police, the old man's demeanour changes drastically. Visibly shaken by this news, he winces in pain, clenching his fists as Olivia watches helplessly. At the heart of this story is a family violently ripped apart by the whims of a merciless tyrant.

PART THREE – Chapter 8 (pp.108–16)

Summary: *Raphael narrates. Jun-Jun reveals his dreams for the future.*

Raphael resumes his narration. He too is apologetic to Olivia for the deception but grateful for her help. Raphael brings the reader up to speed with his actions while Olivia and Gardo were at the prison. Unable to wait, Raphael and Jun-Jun go over José's letter and the newspaper cuttings. Raphael feels a kinship with José, who 'felt like a brother' to him (p.109).

The boys visit the senator's mansion in Green Hills. Jun-Jun has money stashed away for the bus fare, to Raphael's surprise. Demonstrating the developing trust between the boys, Jun-Jun invites Raphael to his home, sharing his savings and revealing his dreams for the future. Jun-Jun's plan is to return home to Sampalo, the island where he was born, 'beautiful as paradise' (p.114), where he can buy a boat and make a living from fishing. He invites Raphael and Gardo to join him, which Raphael contemplates. Raphael feels he will not be safe or welcome at Behala much longer, with suspicion following them at each turn.

Raphael's disposition has shifted dramatically over the course of a few days, the young boy now traumatised and paranoid. 'That time with the police had changed everything,' he reflects, 'people were looking at me strangely, like I'd brought bad luck' (p.115). He is also haunted by the shame of potentially putting his family in danger, something that causes nightmares and bedwetting incidents. The boys know that things will never be the same again, yet they are compelled to keep going.

PART THREE – Chapter 9 (pp.117–26)

Summary: *Jun-Jun narrates. Green Hills lives up to its name.*

This chapter is the first narrated by Jun-Jun, and it serves as a study in contrasts. As the boys take a bus to Green Hills, feeling themselves relax slightly on leaving Behala, they notice the major differences between their living spaces and the senator's area, with its fresh scents and ocean views. They approach Zapanta's house, which is surrounded by large fences and has a gatehouse with armed guards, parklands, ponds, fountains and a golf course. While Jun-Jun fantasises about seeing 'the fat man's ass … roasting like a pig' (p.119), Raphael is more fearful and apprehensive.

Key point

Like the descriptions of Behala and Colva Prison, Mulligan describes living situations as 'stacked', saying that the mansion was 'all stacked up in layers' (p.121). Yet in this case, he draws attention to the lavish opulence of Zapanta's mansion and the wealth he has accumulated at the expense of the poor.

The boys spot a police car and hear a man's voice, causing Raphael to panic and bolt. The voice belongs to a gardener who is more friendly than hostile, suggesting a camaraderie and solidarity among those living on the margins of the wealthy. He shares his cigarette with the boys, mentioning recent media interest in the houseboy who stole millions. The gardener theorises that José Angelico smuggled the money out in an old refrigerator and dumped it at a graveyard.

Confirming his solidarity, the gardener conveys his admiration for José. He declares his hope that 'he gave it away before they killed him', believing that Zapanta, 'that son of a bitch' (p.126), has been stealing from the people for years. There is no love lost between Zapanta and his gardener. Despite working for him for two decades, the gardener has only spoken to him twice, very briefly, in all that time. Just as the senator has contempt for the poor, it is clear the feeling is mutual.

PART THREE – Chapter 10 (pp.127–36)

Summary: *Olivia narrates. This chapter presents more revelations, more corruption and more cryptic clues.*

Olivia's final chapter wraps up the conversation with Gabriel Olondriz, who reveals that José Angelico was one of his many grandchildren. Gabriel's son, Dante Jerome, adopted '13 boys and 19 girls' (p.127) – all children in need. Dante's generosity and selflessness serves as a glaring contrast to a society mostly callously indifferent. Despite his many grandchildren, Gabriel admits that José was a favourite of his, and weeps as he remembers his grandson. He also expresses concern for José's orphaned daughter, Pia Dante.

The entire contents of José's letter are finally revealed to the reader. Gardo, who has memorised it, relays José's tragic last words, including the realisation that he will never be able to see his grandfather again. Yet he also cryptically states that the *'seed-corn'* has been planted and is ready to harvest, and that *'it is accomplished'* (p.130). Upon learning that a code was included with the letter, Gabriel excitedly tells Gardo that its numbers correspond to letters in his Bible. Before he can retrieve the holy text, a prison guard, Marco, quickly wraps up their conversation. Although Marco promises to bring the Bible to Behala later, Gardo knows that they will need to pay a lot of money if they want the Bible turned over to them.

Olivia reveals that Gabriel died peacefully in his sleep soon after they left. She is visited by police who interrogate and threaten her, having been tipped off by Mr Oliva from the prison. Despite her obvious fears, Olivia lies to protect her young friends. Father Juilliard manages to contact Olivia's father, who uses his connections to get her on a plane out of the country immediately, never to return.

Looking back, Olivia tells the boys, 'I left part of my heart in your country' (p.135), listing all the things she has learned in her time at Behala. Despite being confronted with poverty and corruption, her true lesson was a moral one. Though she realises the boys were dishonest, she ends her narration with a conscious paradox: 'thank you so much for using me' (p.136).

Q What types of corruption are emerging here? Do we see one villain or a wider, unjust system at play?

Q Who are the victims of this corruption? What insights are we gaining about the poor and the powerless in this country?

Q How do Gabriel's tender memories of José contradict the media's depiction of him?

Q Why does Olivia conclude her narration with the words 'thank you so much for using me'?

PART FOUR – Chapter 1 (pp.139–47)

Summary: *Jun-Jun narrates. He proves his worth yet again, though not without compromising his conscience in the process.*

Jun-Jun seems proud to tell the reader this section of the story, 'the part where I was the leader' (p.139). Immediately after he and Raphael reunite with Gardo, the boys hear the police arriving, so sneak away. Apprehensive and uncertain of their next steps, Jun-Jun suggests they blend in with the many street kids in Buendia. Although Jun-Jun adapts well, Gardo and Raphael are nervous and plagued with nightmares. What truly distresses them is the knowledge that they can never return to Behala. The boys rent a small room above a laundry to hide in.

Realising that everything hinges on Gabriel's Bible, Gardo tracks down the guard Marco. Marco demands twenty thousand pesos for the Bible, and the boys wonder whether he will really give it to them or if he will turn them in to the authorities. Jun-Jun only has a tenth of the amount saved away and fantasises about getting his hands on Zapanta's stolen millions, saying, 'I wanted that fat pig's money so bad I was aching' (p.143).

Jun-Jun hatches a plan but withholds his idea from the other two, heading back to Behala at midnight as Gardo and Raphael sleep. Wily and resourceful as ever, he hitches a ride in a garbage truck to avoid detection by the police at the dumpsite. Once he arrives, he breaks into the Mission School, and steals money from a safe that Father Juilliard keeps. Jun-Jun wrestles with feelings of shame for robbing his own people and, riddled with guilt, leaves a note for Father Juilliard. Unable to write more than his name, he draws a picture that he hopes Father Juilliard will be able to discern, an illustration of a hug and kisses. He returns to the hideout and slips into bed next to Raphael.

PART FOUR – Chapter 2 (pp.148–52)

Summary: *Gardo narrates. The boys finally get their hands on Gabriel's Bible, after risking their necks yet again.*

With Jun-Jun feeling guilty for stealing the money, the boys decide to donate some of the missing millions to the school. Gardo is still feeling somewhat paranoid and asks himself a series of 'what ifs', imagining the worst-case scenario of the authorities finally catching up with the three boys: 'They would break every bone in all our bodies, slow and mean and loving it' (p.149). Although knowing all too well the potential for violence and death, Gardo resolves never to be captured alive, and is inspired to keep fighting.

The boys meet up with Marco, Gardo taking the lead with the other two shadowing at a distance. Marco produces Gabriel's Bible and Gardo hands over the money. As soon as the transaction is complete, Gardo makes a run for it but is snatched by Marco, proving the boys' fears correct – they have been betrayed. Gardo takes a rubbish-picking hook from his pocket and cuts Marco's face, allowing him to free himself and run. Quiet and nervous no longer, Gardo is unrepentant, declaring, 'I hope his whole cheating face is cut right through, my gift to a filthy traitor' (p.151). He runs past a police officer and doesn't even stop when he hears gunshots. He passes the Bible to Jun-Jun and keeps running until he is safe at the canal. He hopes that his friends are equally unharmed.

This chapter keeps the action in the story moving – it is dramatic, showing how much danger the boys are in, and it builds on the menace of the authority figures in the story.

PART FOUR – Chapter 3 (p.153)

Summary: *Raphael narrates. The boys make another quick getaway, but the police are hot on their heels.*

In this brief chapter, Raphael confirms that he and Jun-Jun are unscathed. Yet he hints that things are about to get worse, for which he feels responsible. Raphael senses that the police have identified him, and the next day, the boys are traced back to their hideout. This builds the suspense for the next chapter: the boys need to take their time to figure out the code, but the reader knows that the police are coming for them, adding tension to what could otherwise have been a more static sequence.

PART FOUR – Chapter 4 (pp.154–8)

Summary: *Raphael narrates. Finally, the code is cracked.*

The three boys are relieved to be reunited in their hideout. They begin decoding the note using Gabriel's Bible. Noticing that someone had written a passage containing the words '*it is accomplished*' (p.155), they work out that several lines have numbers marked that align to Bible verses. Yet the true meaning of the code continues to elude them until midnight, when they are 'slipping into All Souls' Day' (p.156) and Raphael senses the spirits of Gabriel and José guiding them. Realising they need to be reading right to left and not the other way around, they decipher the message: '*Go to the map ref where we lay look for the brightest light my child*' (p.157). Pulling out the map they found with the key and letter, they also realise that the incorrect prisoner number for Gabriel was actually a map coordinate.

Again, the three boys, who lack formal education, have used their intelligence to succeed. The stolen money is located at a graveyard, just as the gardener had theorised. Feeling closer than ever, the boys ponder what the 'brightest light' at a graveyard could possibly be.

PART FOUR – Chapter 5 (pp.159–61)

Summary: *Jun-Jun narrates. The boys are on the run yet again.*

Jun-Jun introduces himself as narrator with his real name, rather than his nickname, implying a newfound sense of maturity. He hears heavy footsteps that signal the authorities are closing in. His impressive survival skills and wily nature are again proven as the boys escape via a hatch in the roof that Jun-Jun had crafted. The police show little consideration for the boys' young ages, more than willing to use force, guns and police dogs to get what they want. Despite their violent efforts, the officers are outrun and outwitted yet again.

PART FOUR – Chapter 6 (pp.162–5)

Summary: *Raphael narrates. The boys escape into a crowd of street kids.*

Raphael reflects on the odds of running for his life twice in a single day, and marvels at Jun-Jun's intuition and cunning. All three boys have proven themselves more than a match for the authorities, escaping their clutches time and again, despite their fears. They traverse several rooftops and jump through windows, arriving at an abandoned, burned-out building that serves as a squat for hundreds of street kids. In a gesture of solidarity, these children cheer them on, helping them blend into the crowds as they hit the streets. They jump into a taxi, heading for Naravo Cemetery.

PART FOUR – Chapter 7 (pp.166–72)

Summary: *Frederico Gonz narrates.*

This chapter is narrated by a man called Frederico who makes memorials for the graveyard. Just like the houses in Behala and the cages at Colva Prison, the graves are built vertically due to the limited space, with up to twenty boxes piled on top of each other.

He tells the reader of his interactions with José Angelico, having met him twice – once each time one of his children died. José requests that the words '*It is accomplished*' (p.167) are chiselled onto the grave of his daughter, Pia Dante. Frederico later comes to realise that José deceived him, although the nature of this deception is withheld from the reader. Despite this, Frederico prays for José when reading of his death in the newspapers. Frederico's insights add to the multiple accounts and recollections of family, friends and associates, all of whom confirm that José was kind and gentle.

The remainder of the chapter consists of a series of four short articles from different newspapers. The first outlines how police are closing in on the missing millions. The article attempts to remain neutral but doesn't shy away from naming Senator Zapanta as a figure of constant speculation and scandal. The second article is more biased, referring to Zapanta as 'much-loved' and a 'great man' (p.170), yet conceding that his governing has not been without controversy. The third piece reads more like a gossip column, using sarcasm to imply that Zapanta is corrupt. The final article, from a student newspaper, demands a change of governance by revolution.

Q In what ways are the boys breaking the rules and even acting against their own moral codes to achieve their goals? Are their intentions pure? Do the ends justify the means?

Q In Part Four, Chapter 5, Raphael states that 'the dead look after you' (p.159). What does he mean by this?

Q What is the impact of the shift from first-person narration to newspaper clippings? What new insights and perspectives are offered here?

PART FIVE – Chapter 1 (pp.175–9)

Summary: *Raphael, Gardo and Jun-Jun all narrate. They visit Naravo Cemetery on the Day of the Dead.*

This is the first chapter narrated by all three boys together. Despite minor conflicts that have occurred throughout their ordeal, the co-authoring here suggests their united front and strong bond.

The taxi journey to the cemetery is prolonged by the crowds celebrating the Day of the Dead. They describe the importance of the festival, as this is meant to be when ghosts visit their loved ones – again foreshadowing the 'ghosts' that help them in the story. The boys notice families marking the occasion together, and the three of them form their own makeshift family also honouring the dead by ensuring that justice is achieved for José Angelico.

Not wanting to draw attention to themselves, they purchase flowers to blend in with the other mourners, and they bribe a guard to help them find José's grave. As daylight dims, Raphael notes how their dirty, grey appearances ironically make them ghost-like themselves. As darkness falls, they see a marble angel that appears pink in the candlelight. As though guided by angels, they climb up a wall to consider their next move and finally see '*the brightest light*' (p.179).

PART FIVE – Chapter 2 (pp.180–6)

Summary: *Raphael, Gardo and Jun-Jun all narrate. At this climactic point of the journey, an important goal is accomplished.*

The boys continue to display a united front via their joint narration in this chapter, the climax of the novel. While sitting on the cemetery wall, they realise the area has been divided into a rich quarter and a poor quarter. Even in death, there is segregation and inequality. Poor people are only able to rent space for their deceased loved ones; if they are unable to continue paying, the bodies are exhumed and thrown in the trash. The bright light they spotted over the wall consists of thousands of mourners coming together in the poor quarter of the cemetery, carrying so many candles the area lights up as though it were daytime.

Key point

The illumination of the area by the faithful, hard-working poorer classes in this chapter symbolically suggests they are the possessors of pure goodness in a city of moral decay.

The boys find the graves of the Angelico family. José's wife, Maria, is buried in a grave bearing the epigraph *'The brightest of lights'* (p.182) and the grave for his daughter, Pia, is inscribed with *'It is accomplished'* (p.183). The boys are saddened by the tragedies that have befallen the Angelico family and feel that breaking open their graves to search for the money would add to this misery. When deciding what to do next, they hear a voice asking what they are looking for. Looking up, instead of a marble angel they see a young girl sitting on one of the stacked graves.

PART FIVE – Chapter 3 (pp.187–8)

Summary: *Raphael, Gardo and Jun-Jun all narrate. A 'ghost' talks.*

In this brief chapter, the girl mentions that she has been waiting for José Angelico to return for over a week. It is unclear whether she has been expecting his spirit to return for the Day of the Dead or if she is unaware of his death. The boys are unsure how to break it to her that he won't be returning. When she calls herself Pia Dante Angelico, standing near the grave with that very name engraved into it, the boys wonder whether they are seeing a ghost.

PART FIVE – Chapter 4 (pp.189–94)

Summary: *Raphael, Gardo and Jun-Jun all narrate. The boys take Pia Dante under their wing, and find the missing money.*

The boys quickly realise that Pia is not a ghost but are moved by how lost, dirty and thin she appears. She is yet another of the forgotten, discarded and helpless street children of the city. Although young themselves, the boys act paternally by using what little cash they have left to feed Pia. Jun-Jun is particularly attentive to her needs, recognising the parallels between them, as both have experienced abandonment and starvation. He sources a place for her to sleep, tenderly tucking her in and attempting to soothe her. The other two boys note that it was 'the only time [they] ever saw Rat cry' (p.191).

Over brandy, they decide on their next move: to find the tools necessary to break open a grave. Knowing that Pia's grave could not contain her remains, they decide it must hold the money. The cemetery is now vacant, as tradition dictates that mourners leave by midnight so the ghosts are left alone. Gardo can sense generations of the dead watching him as they crack the grave open; he feels protected and as though their actions are endorsed. Their theory proves correct, and they discover the money. Raphael tries to describe what six million dollars looks like: 'It looked like change, it looked like the future' (p.194). Knowing it is not their money, they feel guided by the spirits of Gabriel Olondriz and José Angelico.

PART FIVE – Chapter 5 (pp.195–200)

Summary: *Jun-Jun narrates. The boys create a typhoon of cash.*

In this penultimate chapter, Jun-Jun definitively alerts the reader that he is no longer Rat. He is given the reins for this chapter because the boys' next steps were his idea, but he emphatically confirms that all they accomplished was due to them working as a team. Deciding to dump the cash at Behala, they collect Pia and return to their dumpsite home.

Jun-Jun returns the money he stole from Father Juilliard, leaving another note and taking some school uniforms to change into. They head to Jun-Jun's old home and take delight in scattering the remaining money into the winds of the incoming typhoon. Jun-Jun wishes he could watch the dumpsite kids finding the money when they expect to find 'stupp' (p.200). There is pure joy in this moment of altruism: not once do the boys consider keeping the money for themselves. Before leaving, they find another letter from José Angelico, which they take with them as they head to the train station.

PART FIVE – Chapter 6 (pp.201–2)

Summary: *Raphael, Gardo, Jun-Jun and Pia all narrate.*

The three boys conclude the narration, along with their new friend. Speaking from their new location in paradise, Jun-Jun's beloved Sampalo, they express their gratitude to Father Juilliard, Olivia, Grace and Frederico Gonz for helping tell their story. The four spend their days happily fishing, resolved to never tell another lie.

Appendix (pp.203–11)

Mulligan gives the final word to José Angelico in his letter, addressed 'to whom it may concern' (p.203). With his final preoccupation being the wellbeing of his daughter, José's dying wish 'is accomplished' (p.211), as Pia is now safe with her new family.

José notes that Zapanta's biggest mistake was underestimating the poor and, as he outlines precisely how he outsmarted those in power, he reminds the reader that the millions have always belonged to the poor.

Q How are the dead treated by the authorities in the novel? How does this contrast with how their families remember them?

Q Why has Mulligan given the final word to José?

Q Is this an entirely happy ending? Has all corruption and injustice been overcome, and have all perpetrators been held to account?

CHARACTERS & RELATIONSHIPS

Raphael Fernández

Key quotes

'With the right key, you can bust the door wide open. Because nobody's going to open it for you.' (p.9)

'The problem is, your own lies can trap you.' (p.60)

With a name that has religious connotations, being also the name of an archangel, fourteen-year-old Raphael identifies as 'a dumpsite boy' (p.3), having worked at Behala since he was three and 'old enough to move without help and pick things up' (p.5). He lives with his aunt, whom he calls 'Ma', and his younger cousins in the dumpsite, in a makeshift home of two rooms constructed from truck pallets, canvas and plastic. Although Raphael tells the police that he has 'no father' (p.14), there is brief mention of the fact that his father was once in trouble with the law. However, Raphael's parents are now absent or deceased, leading to him taking more responsibility in his family unit, forgoing a formal education to scrounge through the dumpsite to help provide for them.

Despite a hand-to-mouth existence, Raphael never complains or asks for pity. Resigned to his lot in life, he remains enthusiastic and upbeat, with a healthy sense of humour. Raphael is resourceful, turning trash into treasure. He sources plastic to be reused and recycled, and finds tin cans, bottles, rubber and cloth to sell: 'On a good day I'll make two hundred pesos. On a bad, maybe fifty? So you live day to day and hope you don't get sick' (p.6). Raphael's cheerful disposition scarcely hides the risks and challenges associated with a life of abject poverty, as he puts himself in dangerous situations every day. His courage, ingenuity and street smarts are certainly needed when he is tasked with the impossible: exposing and overthrowing one of the most powerful people in the country.

Having no siblings, Raphael's best friend Gardo serves as a substitute brother. The two work at Behala and often share a bed. Although closely bonded, they are conscious of the differences between them. Gardo states, 'Raphael is my best friend but he's like a kid, always laughing, playing, thinking everything's fun, thinking it's a game' (p.27). Despite their differences, they remain loyal and united: 'One thing I know is I'd want [Gardo] on my side, always', Raphael says (p.8). Over the course of the story, Raphael extends his brotherly affection to the orphaned Jun-Jun and Pia.

Raphael's youthful enthusiasm and naivety are more than put to the test. He is open and honest with readers about his fears and anxieties; however, despite these, he remains focused and resolute. Even when faced with intimidation and abuse, and, at one point, physically assaulted and threatened with death, Raphael never wavers in his desire to find the truth, solve the crime and see José Angelico's final wishes realised. Such dedication is testament to his strong moral core and innate sense of right and wrong. Although the situation he is in forces him to lie and be evasive, not only to the police but also to his own aunt, he often wrestles with remorse for this. Ultimately, Raphael can rationalise his actions, atoning for any guilt with acts of selflessness and altruism.

Key point

Although Raphael gets his hands on millions, he never considers keeping all the money for himself, thinking only of the benefits he can bring to the Behala community.

When Father Juilliard first meets Raphael early in the narrative, he describes him as 'shy', with 'long hair over his face' and an 'enchanting smile' (p.51). Over the course of the novel, Raphael's reticence and bashfulness are stripped away to reveal a confident, compassionate and well-adjusted young man. One of the final depictions of Raphael is of him 'crying out he was so happy' (p.199).

Gardo

Key quotes

'People say he's too serious, a boy without a smile …' (Raphael, p.8)

'Oh, my boy, you are – you are an angel. You are a young, sainted angel.' (Gabriel, p.131)

Raphael's partner in crime (and crime-solving), Gardo is practically his twin brother, 'born seven hours ahead ... onto the same sheet' (p.7). Yet, despite their similar ages, Gardo is depicted as more mature and certainly more prudent. His nature is almost diametrically opposite to Raphael's, and he is often cautious and guarded. Even his name implies he is the guardian of his friend. Where Raphael remains cheerful about his circumstances, Gardo is more solemn and realistic. The boys have an intuitive understanding of each other, Raphael stating that 'he always knows what I'm thinking, feeling' (p.7). This intimacy and a steadfast loyalty sustains them when they are thrown into a complex situation that threatens their lives.

Gardo is intelligent, strategising in a way that belies his lack of schooling. Raphael's aunt observes this, telling him, 'Gardo, you're smarter than [Raphael]' (p.34). In several dangerous situations, the boys are saved by Gardo's quick thinking and survival skills. Like Raphael, Gardo also reveals a sense of morality and integrity, apologising for his transgressions. After lying to Olivia, he devotes an entire chapter to asking for forgiveness: 'I was wrong … Please forgive me … I am sorry how it ended for you' (p.103).

Gardo is not afraid to question, challenge or rebuke others. 'The fact that he's older means he pushes me around now and then, tells me what to do,' Raphael concedes, 'and most of the time I let him' (pp.7–8). When Father Juilliard meets the boys for the first time, he remarks that 'you could see at once who the leader was' (p.51). This characteristic strength does not soften or waver over the course of the story. Even in the final chapters, with the mystery resolved and justice mostly achieved, Gardo remains 'firm … you didn't cross Gardo, not to his face' (p.200).

Jun-Jun (Rat)

Key quotes

'... he lived with the rats and had come to look like one.' (Raphael, p.19)

'... wasn't I the hero in the end?' (p.141)

'... we are a team now. Who cares, in the end? Who cares who did what when the whole point was we did it together?' (p.195)

The orphaned Jun-Jun is initially presented as pitiful. He lives alone in a hole among the trash, having previously lived at Central Station. Despite the cramped, squalid conditions, Jun-Jun takes pride in his home, telling Raphael, 'It's the best house I ever had' (p.110). Smaller than the other boys at Behala, he is bullied and mocked: 'A lot of kids would just throw things at him and laugh' (p.23). He is described as 'hungrier than most', with 'arms skinny as pencils' and 'frightened eyes and ... big broken teeth sticking out of his mouth' (p.22).

Such descriptions help explain why he is known as Rat. Yet far from being an insult, the name draws attention to many of Jun-Jun's assets. Just as rats are quick and can 'dive, jump, fly and squirm their way out of anywhere' (p.20), Jun-Jun is agile and wily. His small stature and quick instincts make him an indispensable asset. Without Jun-Jun's contributions, Raphael and Gardo would not have survived their ordeal.

Jun-Jun defies all expectations and preconceptions by continually turning his deficits to his advantage: 'Rat is grey as trash, and he has only the clothes he wears, which are so filthy he can move around and no one sees him' (p.30). As the boys move through the city, dodging the police and various other perils, Jun-Jun helps them stay one step ahead.

Like Raphael and Gardo, Jun-Jun is moral and empathetic. When he steals money from Father Juilliard at the Mission School, he is overcome with guilt, reflecting that he 'felt so low' (p.145) and that 'the shame was making [him] ache' (p.146). Illiterate, Jun-Jun is still able to convey his gratitude and regrets to Father Juilliard in a crudely scribbled drawing, later explaining, 'I hated the thought of you never knowing, and wondering who had so betrayed you, so I drew you a picture … I put lots of 'x's, because I knew people used them as kisses' (pp.146–7). Jun-Jun's first move after finding the stolen millions is to return the money borrowed from the school.

In a rare moment of trust, tenderness and vulnerability, Jun-Jun quietly reveals to Raphael his hopes and dreams for the future: 'Like the secret inside was so big he couldn't say it' (p.113). He reveals he has been diligently saving his money to return to his island home of Sampalo to live as a fisherman. Generously, Jun-Jun invites the boys to share in his dream and Mulligan concludes the novel with this dream realised, as all three boys, along with Pia Dante, arrive on the sandy shores of Sampalo where they 'will fish for ever and live happy lives' (p.202).

In the denouement of the novel, Jun-Jun now insists on being called by his real name, 'no longer Rat' (p.195), a testament to his growing up, asserting himself and reclaiming his identity.

Father Juilliard

Key quotes

'… I have always said that you have to break the rules. I set rules up; then I break them.' (p.48)

'You look at the … children … and it's easy to think what you do in a school like this is of absolutely no consequence or good to anyone.' (p.53)

More than just a narrator, Father Juilliard seems to be the editor and publisher of the boys' story after they depart for Sampalo, announcing to the reader that he is 'the one pulling these accounts together' (p.47). Father Juilliard is the sixty-three-year-old director of the Pascal Aguila Mission School at Behala. He was initially posted to the school to assist with previous mismanagement, only intending to remain for a year. Now in his seventh year overseeing the mission, he has fallen 'in love with the place' (p.47), yet regretfully notes that he is 'being retired this year – partly because of this story' (p.47). This suggests that his final desire before handing the reins to his successor is to set the record straight.

The work of the mission extends beyond education. Father Juilliard provides the children with food, clothes, medicine and access to a bath, while trying to lure them to classes. Infinitely kind, generous and compassionate, Father Juilliard's motivations are genuine – 'you look around at the thousands who cannot be taken care of and it breaks your heart' (p.53) – and he toils to make others' lives better. As a result, the children he is trying to help find it easy to manipulate him, and he notes that 'some of our children are the best liars in the world' (p.84). Yet even as he rebukes himself for being used, he is wise enough not to take it personally, knowing that such deception is merely a tool for survival.

Running the school poses several problems for Father Juilliard. Lack of funding, irregular attendance, stifling heat and precarious, makeshift buildings cause him to wrestle with feelings of inadequacy and futility, as he wonders whether his contributions might be 'of absolutely no consequence or good to anyone' (p.53). He is working within a system and an unjust society that have forced him to be quietly rebellious when needed. Serving as a father figure, his dissenting streak inadvertently inspires the boys to follow suit and to break unjust laws and rules for the greater good.

Olivia Weston

Key quotes

'You're the nicest, kindest mother we ever had here.' (Jun-Jun, p.82)

'I learned perhaps more than any university could ever teach me.' (p.135)

As her surname suggests, Olivia is a Westerner, a young English university graduate who had taken time off to see the world and, like Father Juilliard, had her initial plans derailed when she was seduced by the charms of Behala. Despite being just twenty-two, Olivia refers to herself as the 'temporary house-mother' at Behala's Mission School (p.77). Maternal and kind, she proves 'a good friend' (p.108) to the boys.

Her attachment to Jun-Jun in particular leads her to seek to adopt him. She is deterred by Father Juilliard, who dissuades her partly because of her age – 'a twenty-two-year-old girl from England, wanting to adopt! I told her not to think of it' – and partly because of bureaucracy: 'the machinery for adoption out here is slow' (p.53).

Sensitive and compassionate, Olivia is horrified by the poverty and injustice she is confronted with, saying that it 'makes you want to weep, because it looks so like an awful punishment that will never end' (p.85). Her bleeding heart sees her unwittingly taken for a ride, literally and figuratively, as the boys convince her to escort Gardo to Colva Prison. When the truth is eventually revealed, she curses herself for being so 'stupidly soft-hearted' (p.78). Yet her final narration ends with her saying, 'thank you so much for using me' (p.136), an expression of gratitude that her eyes have been opened to the realities of the world.

José Angelico

Key quote

'… José was kind, gentle, trustworthy and honest.' (Grace, p.72)

Although his character dominates much of the narrative, we never actually meet José Angelico, his life having been tragically ended before the story even begins. Yet his legacy and his unfulfilled ambitions are the catalyst for the boys' quest, and he floats over the story like an angel – as his surname implies. José knew that Senator Zapanta was stealing money earmarked for the poor and decided to steal it back, bravely standing up against corruption and injustice, knowing that it would make him a target. Leaving behind a letter addressed to his daughter, he outlines his motivations – 'my mission was simple, and what I did, I did for you and children like you' (pp.203–4).

Despite the media's negative portrayal of José as a thief, the recollections of those who knew him reinforce his goodness and humanity. His grandfather, Gabriel, confesses that 'José was a favourite … the sweetest boy. He was clever too' (pp.127–8). His colleague,

Grace, refers to him as 'the most trustworthy man … a good man' (pp.72–3) and a headstone engraver he employed testifies that 'he looked to me so meek and so mild' (p.167).

The boys feel inspired by José during challenging times. After courageously resisting the threats and violence made by the police, Raphael wonders, 'Where did I find the strength? I know that it was José Angelico's strength' (p.64). Later he senses the spirit of the martyred man guiding him, saying, 'I also think José was with me' (p.71). On All Saints' Day, the boys again sense his presence, with Jun-Jun stating confidently, 'I have no doubt he's up there [in heaven]' (p.143). Although José Angelico's death was tragic, his influence is immeasurable. Satisfyingly, the novel concludes with his final wishes brought to fruition.

Gabriel Olondriz

Key quote

'The man was not simply weak: he was dying.' (Olivia, p.98)

Another character victimised by corrupt authorities is José Angelico's grandfather, Gabriel. Like his grandson, Gabriel attempted to hold the powerful accountable and was met with the full force of their retribution. The name Gabriel is another reference to an archangel, continuing the allusions to Christianity. Unjustly imprisoned by Senator Zapanta, Gabriel ruminates that the leader 'had many more friends than I, and infinitely more power' (p.102). Making an enemy of Zapanta ultimately earned Gabriel a lifelong prison sentence.

Olivia's initial impressions of Gabriel in prison highlight his frailty: 'His skin was drawn tight, and [his] breathing was so hard. There was a large growth under his jaw, and he seemed to be in pain' (p.98). Gardo tells him of the death of his beloved grandson, which Olivia describes as news that 'fell like a blow … his face was wet and all I could see was pain' (p.107). Gabriel and his kin are revealed to be a loving and tight-knit family ripped apart by amoral and unrepentant forces.

Although clearly suffering, Gabriel is determined to assist Gardo. Gabriel passes away shortly after meeting with Gardo and Olivia, suggesting that he held on just long enough to ensure the truth about his family could emerge. The visit inspires Gardo and the boys, who later feel the man's presence on All Saints' Day, sensing that 'Gabriel Olondriz came and sat beside us' (p.156). They feel protected by the knowledge that 'the dead look after you' (p.159) and even attribute their bursts of energy to Gabriel and his grandson, stating, 'Gabriel and José were still with us ... maybe they'd been pushing that bike with us' (p.197).

Senator Regis Zapanta

Key quote

'... his name was on streets, on a shopping mall in the fancy part of town, and in rising skyscrapers ... He was a big man in every way.' (Raphael, p.109)

Another character who never appears yet looms large is Senator Zapanta. Referred to ironically as 'our trusted vice-president' (p.101), his influence is far-reaching. His enormous size and stature are not just metaphorical; his gardener calls him 'the fattest man I ever saw' (p.123). A newspaper clipping reveals that 'Zapanta campaigned on the slogan, *The brightest smile, the sharpest mind*' (p.172), yet José Angelico, privy to the politician's behaviour behind closed doors, contradicts this in his final letter, condemning his 'frightened mind' and 'false' smiles (p.205).

Zapanta steals public funds allocated to the poorer classes and eliminates anyone who threatens to expose him. Careful not to get his own hands dirty, he instead gets others to commit heinous acts on his behalf. Unsurprisingly, there is no love lost between Zapanta and his citizens. The gardener calls him 'that son of a bitch' (p.126), Jun-Jun fantasises about watching 'the fat man's ass ... roasting like a pig' (p.119) and a student newspaper condemns his '*questionable conscience*', calling for 'a revolution' to overthrow him (p.172). One of the final references to the villain is Jun-Jun calling him the 'senator-vice-president from hell' (p.196).

THEMES, IDEAS & VALUES

Poverty

Key quotes

'... you live day to day and hope you don't get sick.' (Raphael, p.6)

'... you look around at the thousands who cannot be taken care of and it breaks your heart.' (Father Juilliard, p.53)

'Behala is a huge, monstrous, filthy, steaming rubbish dump and you cannot believe human beings are allowed to work there, let alone live there.' (Olivia, p.85)

Mulligan's novel is a fascinating insight into life in a developing country, exploring a part of society that is rarely seen or given a voice. The protagonists in *Trash* live among waste and are in many ways themselves discarded, forced to fend for themselves.

The enormity of Behala engulfs the reader, with vivid descriptions conveying its size and pungency. Behala is compared to the Himalayas, just as vast but far less beautiful. 'It must be about two hundred football pitches big,' Raphael muses (p.4). Its rancid smell is almost palpable, emanating from 'one whole long world of steaming trash' (p.4) containing rubbish that is 'often wet [with] juices [that] are always running' (p.20). In the opening chapter, Raphael declares that 'you can smell Behala long before you see it' (p.4). 'I will never forget the stink,' concurs Olivia (p.85), and even Father Juilliard is taken aback by the stench that sticks to the boys, noticing that 'their smell filled the room' (p.51).

Although the boys never complain about their circumstances, mostly maintaining a cheerful disposition despite their surroundings, foreigners to Behala are more pitying. The English-born Olivia laments the sight of children living and working among the waste, which makes her 'want to weep, because it looks so like an awful punishment that will never end' (p.85), an expression of her innate compassion.

The houses at Behala are essentially makeshift shacks, crudely and precariously constructed out of pallets, canvas and plastic: 'Most of those people live in boxes, and the boxes are stacked up tall and high' (p.3). These tiny, cramped homes are dangerous, yet their inhabitants still face constant threats of eviction as 'every now and again the homes get torn down and the people get shipped out' (p.36). One of Mulligan's motifs throughout the novel is the image of poor people literally living on top of one another. Raphael's home is 'stacked over three families below' (p.16) and, when forced to flee their homes, the boys end up in 'a tiny room … high up in a stack of old shacks over a laundry … not much bigger than a coffin' (p.140). In Colva Prison, 'cages were stacked three high' (p.93) and in the poor people's section of Naravo Cemetery, 'the dead get stacked up in boxes' (p.180). Even in death, the less fortunate are crammed together.

Key point

Mulligan deliberately portrays the cells of the prison as similar to the homes in Behala. In both, we see evidence of the poor being treated appallingly, discarded and forgotten.

Behala residents face daily risks living and working among the waste. Raphael's chosen turf is among giant bulldozers and cranes, where 'you're not supposed to work … because it's dangerous' (p.7). The spectre of the Smoky Mountain tragedy looms large, a disaster involving piles of garbage collapsing in on themselves at a similar site, resulting in 'nearly a hundred killed' (p.22).

These mountains of waste are also a commentary on a consumerist and wasteful society, which is highlighted by how much of the dumpsite's contents can be reused, repurposed or sold. Gardo revels in the waste from the wealthier area of town, noting, 'McKinley trash is good-quality trash: food, newspaper, a lot of plastic and glass' (p.30). The boys are resourceful, scouring the waste with their hooks in search of items of value. In Part One, Chapter 1, Raphael lists all the potential treasures he seeks: 'plastic can be turned into cash, fast … tin cans – anything metal

... glass ... rubber is good' (p.5). Gardo later confirms, 'we get money for what we can sell' (p.27). The boys are practical, quick-witted and smart, having been forced to learn essential life skills from an early age.

Because many people in the city don't have access to a toilet, the Behala inhabitants live among human excrement, colloquially referred to in the novel as 'stuppa' or 'stupp'. 'There's a lot of things hard to come by in our sweet city,' Raphael notes, and 'one of the things too many people don't have is toilets and running water' (p.3). Thus, residents have no choice but to dispose of their waste any way they can, leading to many unpleasant revelations for those wading through the garbage each day.

To make matters worse, the Behala inhabitants also find themselves living among rats – 'the trash is alive at night: that's when the rats come out' (p.20). Jun-Jun even refers to the rats as his friends, leading others to bestow him a nickname in their honour 'because he lived with the rats and had come to look like one' (p.19). Later, Olivia draws parallels between all the Behala children and the scurrying vermin they share their homes with, reflecting, 'you sometimes think they have pretty much the same life' (p.85).

Olivia's observation reveals a wider societal perception that can be somewhat patronising and, at its worst, demeaning. When Raphael is detained by the police, we are given insight into how the authorities look down on the poor. Although only a child, he is belittled, referred to as 'a piece of shit' (p.62) and 'scum' (p.65) for having come from Behala, and told, 'You stink of it ... of garbage ... boy, that's all you are' (p.66). Seeing people as trash makes it easier for those in power to dehumanise them. The police threaten Raphael, telling him, 'We could put you in the trash and nobody would care' (p.65). Despite his youth, Raphael seems familiar with this disparaging sense of superiority, noting, 'I could see he was weighing me, looking me over, wondering what, if anything, I was worth. Valuable or trash?' (p.67). The irony in Mulligan's novel is that those discarded by society triumph in the end, revealing themselves to be more moral and decent than those afforded privilege and position.

Power and corruption

Key quotes

'When the police get mean, you don't want to be around.' (Gardo, p.29)

'... everybody siphons a little bit here, a little bit there.' (Gabriel, p.104).

'He's spent more than three decades lining his pockets, and his main achievement is that he's made the country's poor feel worthless and powerless.' (*Daily Star* report, p.172)

The widespread poverty depicted in the novel is largely the result of an unjust system designed to benefit the rich and powerful at the expense of the lower classes. Many in positions of authority turn out to be self-serving and corrupt, both morally and literally. Thus the rich in Mulligan's novel seem to get richer while the poor are invisible and dispensable.

Mulligan portrays the cynicism of local politicians who prefer the optics of helping the poor over taking meaningful action, as when Behala saw 'four police cars come on an election visit, surrounding a man who wanted to be mayor – lights flashing ... they all love a show' (p.10). The Vice President also uses the poor as a prop, for example in 'a dramatic poster campaign aimed at the illiterate, featuring laughing orphans holding placards that spelled out his name', and when hypocritically 'campaign[ing] for wider education, whilst presiding over an education budget that has dwindled by 18% over two years' (p.170). This obsession with self-promotion explains how even uneducated children living in a dumpsite are aware of him, as his ubiquitous name 'was on streets, on a shopping mall in the fancy part of town, and in rising skyscrapers' (p.109).

Although he doesn't directly appear in the narrative, Senator Zapanta is depicted as an immoral and brazen criminal. The novel's villain, he is motivated by greed and has 'spent more than three decades lining his pockets' (p.172). In contrast with the impoverished world of Behala, his residence is striking, a gated mansion complete with golf courses, rolling green lawns, ponds and fountains. Jun-Jun's stunned reaction on entering the grounds speaks volumes: 'I had never seen anything like it ... a palace, for the king' (p.121). Zapanta's ostentatious wealth and greed are accentuated by Mulligan's references to his obesity and swine-like qualities. He is described as 'a big man in every way' (p.109), the 'fattest man [the gardener] ever saw' (p.123) and a 'fat pig' (p.143).

The Vice President is 'constantly dogged by accusations and scandal' (p.169), and the crime at the heart of *Trash* is the embezzlement of public funds earmarked for the poorer classes: 'thirty million dollars of international aid money ... a package of grants ... to build hospitals and schools' (p.102). This culture of theft starts at the top and permeates all aspects of society. Zapanta is not alone in stealing public funds, as the reference to 'three senators who'd been siphoning off public taxes and stowing them off-shore' (p.50) indicates. Even lowly prison staff are lining their pockets. Gardo and Olivia are only granted access to Gabriel at Colva Prison because 'the money you paid bribes the administration here' (p.100). The world in *Trash* revolves around money. This culture of self-preservation and survival has turned everyone into opportunists, hustlers and bargain-seekers – even the Behala boys and Central Station street kids exchange money in return for information or access.

However, those in power have significant advantages and can get others to do their dirty work. Zapanta, who trained as a lawyer, uses his background to silence those who challenge him, 'notoriously quick to challenge and in many cases prosecute critics of his policies and personal conduct' (p.169). Violence is also used to intimidate and to stamp out dissent. The police serve as the lackeys of the powerful, terrorising and threatening anyone who stands in their way. The boys of Behala bitterly recollect their experiences in dealing with the authorities, saying, 'when the police get mean, you don't want to be around' (p.29) and believing that 'they would break every bone in all our bodies, slow and mean and loving it' (p.149). Olivia's descriptions of the children imprisoned at Colva Prison support Raphael's testimonials of the strong arm of the law coming down hard on the young – 'everyone knows stories about what happens to kids if they get caught breaking the law

... the prisons take kids quicker than they take men' (pp.40–1). The horrific scenes of the young Raphael being beaten and intimidated are a reminder of the extent to which the police will go to maintain authority and control. Raphael describes his treatment graphically, stating, 'I tried to wipe my face, but it was all blood and snot, and I was slapped again, hard, so that lights were flashing ... The policeman was leaning over me, one big hand on the table, one hand twisting my hair' (p.61). Although Raphael is lucky to escape the murderous clutches of the police, he reminds us that José Angelico entered a similar police station for an interview and, tragically, was never seen alive again.

José is not the only character in *Trash* who attempted to stand up against this widespread culture of corruption. The Pascal Aguila Mission School at Behala is named in honour of a citizen and freedom fighter 'who fought corruption and was shot to death for his pains' (p.49). Aguila worked to improve life for the impoverished and to hold the powerful to account, only to find himself on the receiving end of 'twenty-six bullets – the same calibre as a policeman's gun, and his murderers were never found' (p.50). The boys from Behala carry on the legacies of both deceased men, working against the powerful despite seemingly insurmountable obstacles and risks to their own safety. Their inherent goodness and unwavering commitment to the truth is starkly juxtaposed with the unscrupulous and corrupt government.

Deception and guilt

Key quotes

'They had all got what they wanted, and had deceived me beautifully.' (Father Juilliard, p.54)

'The problem is, your own lies can trap you.' (Raphael, p.60)

'And I laughed, because it occurred to me – there and then – that the garbage boy had just lied his way out from under the noses of those clever men.' (Raphael, p.69)

The government portrayed in *Trash* is extremely corrupt and the novel shows the extent to which those in power will go to conceal their dishonesty. What is revealed to readers is a system built on deception and the novel demonstrates how challenging it can be to uncover the truth. Yet it also focuses on the little white lies people tell without malicious or selfish intent, and often with the aim of achieving justice.

The young protagonists often conceal their true intentions and are frequently forced into situations where they need to lie or else face horrific consequences. These lies are yet another survival skill learned by the boys: one that they rarely, if ever, use for selfish reasons in the novel. Father Juilliard later comments that some of the children at the school 'are the best liars in the world'. Yet he is quick to realise that this dishonesty stems from a lack of choice, acknowledging that 'it is survival' (p.84). The underlying causes for such an instinct are an understandable distrust of the authorities, concerns for the safety of loved ones and genuine fear and panic. The lies told by Raphael, Gardo and Jun-Jun are revealed to be a form of self-preservation practised by otherwise moral and compassionate characters.

This idea is first established when the police visit Behala to ascertain the whereabouts of José Angelico's possessions. It is significant that Raphael's first impulse is to withhold what he knows: 'I needed time to think, so I stood there, dumb' (p.12). Raphael instinctively knows not to trust the police and their empty promises. What sets Raphael and Gardo apart from the dishonest, unrepentant authorities are their consciences and their integrity. Often when they find themselves embroiled in a lie, they wrestle with guilt. When Raphael's aunt confronts the boys about their falsehoods, Gardo admits, 'All I could think about was the lies, stacking up now, and how I hoped it was worth it' (p.33).

Knowing that his lies placed enormous scrutiny and strain on his family, Raphael wrestles with his guilty conscience, frankly stating that he is 'ashamed' (p.115). The first-person narration offers an opportunity for characters to come clean to the readers, and Raphael bravely reveals that he 'was having nightmares and waking up crying' (p.115). Later,

Jun-Jun recollects how Raphael's guilt, as well as his trauma, had manifested in more sleepless nights, having observed his friend crying at night 'for his auntie and his cousins' (p.141).

Jun-Jun himself experiences similar pangs of guilt when he is forced to steal money from the Mission School safe, noting in a moment of self-reflection, 'It would be robbing from your own people, which is why I felt so low' (p.145) and that 'the shame was making me ache' (p.146). Jun-Jun tries to assuage his conscience by drawing a picture for Father Juilliard that he hopes will explain his actions. When Senator Zapanta's stolen millions are recovered, Jun-Jun is quick to return his borrowed funds directly to the Mission School.

When the boys deceive Olivia to gain access to Colva Prison, she is initially bothered, cursing her own 'vanity and stupidity … the fact that three little boys could break [her] heart one minute and flatter [her] the next, all the time lying and lying' (p.82). Yet once her eyes are opened to the noble reasons for the deceit – the pursuit of justice and the desire to prioritise her safety – she is surprisingly grateful, and she ends her narration with the sign-off, 'thank you so much for using me' (p.136). Still, the boys are remorseful for having manipulated her. Gardo devotes an entire chapter to his penitence, declaring, 'I am so sorry for what I did … Please forgive me' (p.103) and Raphael later follows suit, saying, 'I am so sorry for deceiving you, Sister' (p.108). Before Olivia leaves the country, she lies to the police herself, withholding what she learned from Gabriel Olondriz at the prison, suggesting she has learned that lying is a necessary evil to prevent more evil.

Knowing that the authorities cannot be trusted, Raphael lies when required, even in the face of immense danger and threats to his life. Faced with a terrorising interrogation, he doubles down and withholds the truth from the police, even going so far as to 'swear to God' and to his 'mother's soul' (p.60). Raphael seems to justify this deception as a form of retribution and one-upmanship, gleefully rejoicing in how he outwitted the police, even laughing because 'the garbage boy had just lied his way out from under the noses of those clever men' (p.69). Yet, in a moment of self-awareness and insight, Raphael warns readers that 'your own lies can trap you' (p.60) and to be careful not to make a habit out of dishonesty for fear of the eventual consequences.

Key point

Note that once the crime is solved, justice has been at least partially upheld, and the boys have retreated safely to their island paradise, they conclude their joint narration by plainly stating that 'the lying is finished' (p.202). Just as Olivia forgives the boys, we as readers can also excuse their stretching of the truth to achieve a greater good.

Friendship and solidarity

Key quotes

'One thing I know is I'd want him on my side, always.' (Raphael on Gardo, p.8)

'When one of their number is hurt, everyone feels the wound.' (Olivia, p.79)

At the heart of the novel is the story of three young boys who work together, united by a shared goal. Although they certainly question and challenge one another in the face of immense stress, Raphael, Gardo and Jun-Jun remain steadfastly loyal to and supportive of one another. Even when the pressure becomes intense, they don't crack and never once turn on, or turn their backs on, each other. This commitment serves them well, helping them to combine their individual strengths to outwit the authorities and to survive several attempts on their lives. As Gardo emphatically declares, 'I say stick together. We ought to stay together in this' (p.39).

Jun-Jun has a few brief moments of self-congratulation, asserting himself and seeking recognition and validation for his contributions, admitting that 'Gardo says all I do is brag and take credit' (p.197). Yet in the denouement of *Trash*, he ultimately eschews pride to proclaim, 'Who cares who did what when the whole point was we did it together?' (p.195).

Raphael and Gardo's intimacy has existed since birth; they have spent years working side by side and often slept in the same bed. Raphael says of Gardo, 'He's not my brother but he might as well be' (p.7) and Gardo later refers to Raphael as 'my friend and brother' (p.191). This sense of kinship is extended to Jun-Jun, and later to Pia Dante and even to the deceased José Angelico, of whom Raphael states, 'He felt like a brother to me now' (p.109). The three protagonists laugh together, fret together and scheme together at every step of their journey, escaping the city in the end, with Pia Dante, as a tight, makeshift family ready to embark on the rest of their lives collectively.

The residents of the Behala neighbourhood also seem to value each other, suggesting that the boys' loyalty and commitment was learned at home. Despite the daily grind of poverty, the community seems united by a sense of decency, empathy and compassion. The residents emerge from their slums to engage in communal meals at which 'there was music and singing, and everyone was happy' (p.32). Raphael's aunt is depicted cooking dinner for thirty people, a testament to a caring, maternal nature that extends beyond her own children to her nephew, his friends and the entire Behala community. Raphael cheerfully explains that 'if you had no parents, you had aunties or uncles, or older brothers, or cousins, and so there was always somebody who would take care of you and give you a bit of the mat to sleep on, and a plate of rice' (p.19).

One reason Olivia is so taken by Behala is its people and their sense of camaraderie and selflessness. Father Juilliard teaches the Behala children the lessons of Pascal Aguila, the school's namesake, who died trying to ensure the poor were taken care of, telling them that 'his picture hangs over the altar. He was a man determined to build things and make life better' (p.49). Aguila worked to ensure squatters were protected, that workers' safety was paramount and that hospitals set up a unit for the poor.

This sense of unity and solidarity is also depicted by Mulligan in other scenes, from the station boys working together, to Senator Zapanta's servants, to the street kids who cheer the boys on as they run from the clutches of the police – 'they were wild for us. We all ran together ... everyone was screaming and laughing, shouting' (pp.163–4). Collectively, the novel paints a portrait of an inherently moral underclass who relate to each other's shared struggles, supporting and encouraging one another. Even those incarcerated at Colva Prison display a sense of community and humanity despite the inhumane conditions they are forced to endure. As Olivia walks through the jail, she is taken by their 'cheerful cries – friendly cries, and so much laughter' (p.93), even though they are being treated like animals. Their core decency – they call her 'ma'am' and are 'so well mannered' (p.95) – contrasts starkly with the behaviour of the authorities, who only look after themselves. Mulligan even has his characters believe that their solidarity and devotion extends to the hereafter; for example, when Jun-Jun states that 'the dead look after you' (p.159).

DIFFERENT INTERPRETATIONS

Different interpretations arise from different responses to a text. Over time, a text will evoke a wide range of responses from its readers, who may come from various social or cultural groups and live in very different places and historical periods. Responses by critics and reviewers can be published in newspapers, journals and books, both online and in print. They can also be expressed in discussions among readers in the media, classrooms, book groups and so on.

While there is no single correct reading or interpretation of a text, it is important to understand that an interpretation is more than a personal opinion – it is the justification of a point of view on the text. To present an interpretation of a text based on your point of view, you must use a logical argument and support it with relevant evidence from the text.

Critical viewpoints

Mulligan's novel was met with critical acclaim upon its release and continues to be popular with readers and educators more than a decade later. This has not made the text immune from controversy, however. In 2010, *Trash* was initially shortlisted for the Blue Peter Book Awards, which were annual awards for children's literature. However, the honour was then revoked on the grounds that the novel was unsuitable for younger readers because of its violence and coarse language. Mulligan defended his work, criticising those who wanted to shelter young people from the confronting yet important realities of the world.

Another debate stems from Mulligan's choice to set his story in a country other than his own. Some critics have questioned the appropriateness of Mulligan, an English-born writer, commenting on the social problems of a developing country. Like the character of Olivia Weston in the novel, a well-intentioned but privileged outsider engaging in 'voluntourism', a questionable practice that may do more harm than good, Mulligan could be accused of naivety at best and of exhibiting a 'white saviour' sense of smug superiority at worst. Mulligan never explicitly mentions the name of the country in which his story is set, which potentially allows him to sidestep accusations from Filipino people who may be displeased that an English person is painting their country in an unflattering light.

Two interpretations

Interpretation 1: *Trash* is a bleak portrayal of poverty and injustice.

Andy Mulligan's bildungsroman novel *Trash* depicts the adventures of three impoverished 'rubbish boy[s]' (p.4) who outsmart the authorities in order to solve a mystery. Yet beneath its lively narrative about likeable young protagonists working together as amateur sleuths lies a grim story of misfortune and adversity. Mulligan does not shy away from realistic descriptions of poverty, suffering and violence due to an unjust and corrupt social system. The novel bleakly reveals how the lower classes can be as discarded and unwanted as trash, as the novel's title suggests.

Trash exposes how underprivileged people in developing countries are forced to endure a hand-to-mouth existence in inconceivable squalor. The young protagonists live and work at the Behala landfill, 'a huge, monstrous, filthy, steaming rubbish dump' (p.85) that 'must be about two hundred football pitches big' (p.4). Forced to rummage through trash to make a living, they work alongside countless rats and sift through human excrement, which they call 'stupp'. Foreigner Olivia Weston incredulously states that 'you cannot believe human beings are allowed to work there, let alone live there', describing such an existence as 'an awful punishment that will never end' (p.85). Their homes are nothing more than shanties made from flimsy materials and lacking basic amenities. The children from these lower classes forgo a traditional education simply to survive, yet still struggle to find enough to eat. All the young characters are portrayed as malnourished, with Gardo described as 'thin as a whip' (p.7), Jun-Jun depicted as 'so thin it was like he was just straws and paper' (p.39) and Pia said to be 'so weak she could hardly stand up' (p.189). Mulligan's vivid depictions of Behala and its inhabitants serve as a harsh criticism of a wasteful, uncaring consumerist society.

Living in such an unjust world forces the young protagonists of *Trash* to put themselves in danger every day. The mountains of unstable piles of rubbish at Behala present innumerable hazards, with Raphael conceding that 'working under the trash as it's raining down … that is *very* dangerous' (p.7). The citizens know all too well the possibility of a painful death when traversing such precarious landscapes, recalling the Smoky Mountain tragedy in which 'there were nearly a hundred killed' (p.22). Yet the more immediate risks come from their dealings with the authorities. The police threaten, terrorise and abuse those who get in their way, even using physical force on children; for example, Gardo believes that the police 'would break every bone in all our bodies, slow and mean and loving it' (p.149). In one confronting scene, Raphael is apprehended and interrogated by the police, who punch, kick and choke him, and even dangle him from a window. Depressingly, the cruel and unrepentant authorities never face any consequences for their actions. Mulligan's bleak depiction of life at Behala is somewhat dystopian, revealing the dangerous and even deadly conditions in which some people are forced to live.

The poverty shown in the novel can be directly attributed to corrupt and unjust authorities who are elected to care for their citizens, yet only work to enrich themselves. The Vice President, Senator Zapanta, campaigned using propaganda 'featuring laughing orphans holding placards that spelled out his name' (p.170) only to forget about the needy once he was elected. Zapanta lives a life of luxury, having 'spirited away thirty million dollars of international aid money' (p.102), and has 'made the country's poor feel worthless and powerless' (p.172). Once in command, Zapanta abuses his authority to maintain his lofty position, stamping out dissent and imprisoning and even callously murdering anyone who stands in his way. The spectres of Pascal Aguila and José

Angelico haunt the narrative, with the former getting 'twenty-six bullets' (p.50) and the latter 'smashed apart by police' (p.147), all under the orders of corrupt authorities. Although the mystery within the novel is eventually resolved, we do not see Zapanta or others who misuse their power face any consequences for their actions. By resisting this satisfying resolution, Mulligan cynically suggests that corruption and abuse will always prevail. With references to other elected officials 'siphoning off public taxes and stowing them off-shore' (p.50), Mulligan suggests that such problems are much more widespread than just one individual. Even if Zapanta were held to account, this would not automatically solve the deeply ingrained systemic injustice depicted in Mulligan's bleak novel.

Despite its happy ending, Mulligan's novel leaves readers with a bleak and disheartening portrait of the unspeakable hardships the poorer classes are forced to endure while the powerful live lives of ease obtained through dishonesty and cruelty. By never naming the city or country in which *Trash* is set, Mulligan reminds us that such stories exist in all reaches of the globe.

Interpretation 2: *Trash* is an inspiring tale of triumph over adversity.

Andy Mulligan's novel *Trash* is set in the slums of Behala and depicts the lives of three boys, Raphael, Gardo and Jun-Jun, who are forced to scavenge through garbage just to survive. While depicting an immoral and corrupt world that poses huge challenges for the characters, the story is ultimately an uplifting and inspiring depiction of underdogs succeeding despite the odds. The protagonists' resilience, determination and fundamental decency enables them to solve a crime, fulfil the wishes of a murder victim and give back to their own community. The novel ends triumphantly, championing friendship, resilience and morality – the true treasure among the trash.

The community of Behala is depicted positively, demonstrating how care and compassion can exist even against a backdrop of dire poverty. Despite their challenging circumstances, the residents refuse to succumb to despair, maintaining a sense of humour even in their bleak surroundings. Raphael seems somewhat proud to announce himself as a 'dumpsite boy' (p.3), narrating his chapters in a lively, enthusiastic manner. Even when living in squalor, the community is portrayed as connected, upbeat and vibrant, with 'music and singing … everyone was happy' (p.32). Raphael's aunt cooks for the community, supporting her nephew's observation that at Behala 'there was always somebody who would take care of you and give you a bit of the mat to sleep on, and a plate of rice' (p.19). The residents take care of their own, despite their desperate existence. They 'don't usually steal from each other' (p.10) but come together to support and care for neighbours and friends. These qualities lead English volunteer Olivia Weston to declare that she 'fell in love' (p.78) with Behala, observing how 'when one of their number is hurt, everyone feels the wound' (p.79). Underpinning their challenging existence is a sense of community, compassion and selflessness that is inspiring.

The boys' ability to outwit the authorities in their quest for justice is equally impressive. Despite a lack of formal education, they ultimately achieve their goals. The police constantly follow and harass the boys, often using violence to intimidate and obstruct them. Yet time and again, Raphael, Gardo and Jun-Jun are able to deflect them with half-truths and outrun them. Raphael takes satisfaction from this, laughing at his ability to escape 'from under the noses of those clever men' (p.69). Yet what motivates the boys is the desire for justice and the fulfilment of José Angelico's dying wishes. The boys convey true compassion for the murdered man, with Raphael saying, 'God rest his poor soul' (p.70), and strive to ensure his death was not in vain. In times of hardship, Raphael draws inspiration from José, commenting that 'José was with me' (p.71) and saying, 'Where did I find the strength? I know that it was José Angelico's strength' (p.64). In his depictions of the young outwitting the powerful, Mulligan demonstrates how justice can be achieved despite the odds.

At its heart, *Trash* is an uplifting story of friendship and solidarity. In the face of poverty, violence and various other obstacles, the three friends remain resolute and loyal, working together to achieve their goals. When strategising early in the novel, Gardo announces to the other two, 'I say stick together' (p.39) and they remain true to this request. At the novel's denouement, when they are revelling in their success, Jun-Jun affirms that 'the whole point was we did it together' (p.195). The three support each other at every turn and draw strength from their bond, which transcends friendship to become a profound sense of brotherhood. This closeness and solidarity is reflected in Mulligan's choice to have all three boys narrating together in the final chapters, using inclusive language in the final lines: 'We will fish for ever and live happy lives. That is our plan, and nothing will stop us' (p.202).

Although the novel confronts the reader with its striking depictions of adversity and injustice, the story concludes with real hope and happiness. Good trumps evil, justice is partially restored, and our protagonists are safe and content in their new home. Mulligan's story is a testament to the triumph of the human spirit, revealing a tale of community, solidarity and true friendship.

QUESTIONS & ANSWERS

This section focuses on your own analytical writing on the text, and gives you strategies for producing high-quality responses in your coursework and exam essays.

Essay writing – an overview

An essay on a literary work is a formal and serious piece of writing that presents your point of view on the text, usually in response to a given topic. Your 'point of view' in an essay is your interpretation of the meaning of the text's language, structure, characters, situations and events, supported by detailed analysis of textual evidence.

Analyse – don't summarise

In your essays it is important to avoid simply summarising what happens in a text.

- A **summary** is a description or paraphrase (retelling in different words) of the characters and events. For example: 'Macbeth has a horrifying vision of a dagger dripping with blood before he goes to murder King Duncan.'
- An **analysis** is an explanation of the real meaning or significance that lies 'beneath' the text's words (and images, for a film). For example: 'Macbeth's vision of a bloody dagger shows how deeply uneasy he is about the violent act he is contemplating, and conveys his sense that supernatural forces are impelling him to act.'

A limited amount of summary is sometimes necessary to let your reader know which part of the text you wish to discuss. However, always keep this to a minimum and follow it immediately with your analysis of what this part of the text is really telling us.

Plan your essay

Carefully plan your essay so that you have a clear idea of what you are going to say. The plan ensures that your ideas flow logically, that your argument remains consistent and that you stay on topic. An essay plan should be a list of **brief dot points** covering no more than half a page.

- Include your central argument or main contention – a concise statement of your overall response to the topic.
- Write three or four dot points for each paragraph, indicating the main idea and evidence/examples from the text. In your essay you will need to *expand* on these points and *analyse* the evidence.

Structure your essay

An essay is a complete, self-contained piece of writing. It has a clear beginning (the introduction), middle (several body paragraphs) and end (the last paragraph or conclusion). It must also have a central argument that runs throughout, linking each paragraph to form a coherent whole. See examples of introductions and conclusions in the 'Analysing a sample topic' and 'Sample answer' sections.

The introduction establishes your overall response to the topic. It includes your main contention and outlines the main evidence you will refer to in the course of the essay. Write your introduction *after* you have done a plan and *before* you write the rest of the essay.

The body paragraphs argue your case – they present evidence from the text and explain how this evidence supports your argument. Each body paragraph needs:

- a strong **topic sentence** (usually the first sentence) that states the main point being made in the paragraph
- **evidence** from the text, including some brief quotations
- **analysis** of the textual evidence, with **explanation** of its significance and how it supports your argument
- **links back to the topic** in one or more statements, usually towards the end of the paragraph.

Connect the body paragraphs so that your discussion flows smoothly. Use some linking words and phrases such as 'similarly' and 'on the other hand', though don't start every paragraph like this. Another strategy is to use a significant word from the last sentence of one paragraph in the first sentence of the next.

Use key terms from the topic – or synonyms for them – throughout, so the relevance of your discussion to the topic is always clear.

The conclusion ties everything together and finishes the essay. It includes strong statements that emphasise your central argument and provide a clear response to the topic.

Avoid simply restating the points made earlier in the essay – this will end on a very flat note and imply that you have run out of ideas and vocabulary. The conclusion should be a logical extension of what you have written, not just a repetition or summary of it. Writing an effective conclusion can be a challenge. Try using these tips.

- Start by linking back to the final sentence of the second-last paragraph, rather than leaping to your main contention straight away – this helps your writing to flow.
- Use synonyms and expressions with equivalent meanings to vary your vocabulary. This allows you to reinforce your line of argument without being repetitive.
- When planning your essay, think of one or two broad statements or observations about the text's wider meaning. These should be related to the topic and your overall argument. Keep them for the conclusion, since they will give you something 'new' to say but still follow logically from your discussion. The introduction will be focused on the topic, but the conclusion can present a wider view of the text.

Essay topics

1. 'So you live day to day and hope you don't get sick.'
   The residents of Behala lead challenging and hopeless lives.
   Do you agree?
2. 'I came to learn a few things about Rat that I had never known and never asked about.'
   What do the characters learn about themselves and others in *Trash*?
3. In *Trash*, Andy Mulligan portrays a clear distinction between malicious deceit and dishonesty for a moral purpose.
   Discuss.
4. 'I say stick together. We ought to stay together in this.'
   The boys in *Trash* succeed through unity and solidarity.
   Discuss.
5. What is the impact of having multiple narrators in *Trash*?
6. 'With the right key, you can bust the door wide open. Because nobody's going to open it for you.'
   The protagonists in *Trash* control their own destiny.
   Do you agree?
7. At its heart, *Trash* is a story about good triumphing over evil.
   Discuss.
8. The adults in *Trash* are all selfish and corrupt.
   To what extent do you agree?
9. 'I learned that the world revolves around money.'
   To what extent does *Trash* endorse this statement?
10. *Trash* portrays the idea that the rich and powerful will always triumph.
    Discuss.

Vocabulary for writing on *Trash*

Bildungsroman: a coming-of-age story; from a German word that combines the words for 'education' and 'novel'.

Climax: the highest point of tension in a narrative.

Denouement: the final section of a narrative, where the various threads of the story are resolved.

First-person narration: a story told from a character's point of view.

Analysing a sample topic

Andy Mulligan's novel suggests that there are always treasures among the trash.
To what extent do you agree?

This question asks you to at least consider challenging the topic. You can agree, disagree or partly agree. In this case, at least partly disagreeing may allow you to demonstrate a broader understanding of the text. Ensure your contention is clearly expressed in your introduction and explain the reasons for your view.

- The key words here are 'treasures' and 'trash'. How do you define these terms? What synonyms could you substitute here to avoid sounding repetitive?
- Is the topic referring to literal trash and treasure? Or can we apply these terms metaphorically?
- What does Raphael say about finding treasure in the very first chapter?
- What is treasured by the characters? As well as material things, consider qualities, aspirations, morals etc.

The following is one way to tackle this topic; there is no single 'correct' interpretation. As long as you explicitly respond to the topic and link all your arguments and evidence back to it, there are multiple approaches you could take.

Sample introduction

> 'Maybe one day you'll find something nice … then one day I did.' In Andy Mulligan's coming-of-age novel, *Trash*, Raphael Fernández discovers a key that eventually rips his entire world open, declaring that 'with the right key, you can bust the door wide open'. Raphael himself admits that such finds are rare. At Behala, the enormous rubbish dump where he lives and works, much of what exists are 'piles of steaming trash' and 'human muck'. Yet both within and beyond the mountains of trash lie treasures, real and metaphorical, that are capable of changing everything.

Body paragraph outline

Paragraph 1: Raphael, a 'dumpsite boy', declares that the treasures among the trash are few and far between.

- Through Raphael's lively first-person commentary, we learn of his job as a scavenger.
- Raphael mocks those who ask whether he ever finds nice things, 'Friend, I think I know what I find … *stuppa*'.
- Raphael's descriptions of Behala on page 4 create an impression of enormous waste and pungent, rancid smells.
- Olivia Weston also confirms the squalid conditions of Behala in her observations on page 85.

Paragraph 2: However, Raphael and the other Behala scavengers use their ingenuity to reuse and resell items of value.

- Raphael outlines all the items that 'can be turned into cash, fast' on page 5 – plastic, paper, tin, glass, rubber etc.
- The boys' ingenuity and resourcefulness are demonstrated by their ability to discern items of value, even within the hazardous conditions of the dumpsite.
- They use the money earned to provide for their families.
- By describing the extreme amounts of waste in Behala, and noting that much of it can be reused, Mulligan critiques societies that consume excessively and create so much unnecessary waste.

Paragraph 3: Moral and humane people are the real treasures of Behala.

- Even on the very first page, Raphael sarcastically yet affectionately refers to Behala as 'our sweet city'.
- The community takes care of one another: Raphael notes that 'there was always somebody who would take care of you and give you a bit of the mat to sleep on, and a plate of rice' and Olivia observes, 'when one of their number is hurt, everyone feels the wound'.
- The boys show themselves to be moral and empathetic, never once considering keeping the found money all to themselves.
- They give back to their community: 'the notes spilled out and whirled, and it was a storm of money'.

Sample conclusion

> In *Trash*, Mulligan confirms the adage that appearances are often deceptive. Although living in a world that is often pungent, ugly and unjust, the characters of Behala emerge as the real treasures to be found among the trash – kind, considerate and caring in an often cruel and corrupt world.

SAMPLE ANSWER

What is the impact of having multiple narrators in *Trash*?

Andy Mulligan's young adult novel *Trash* interlaces several different perspectives to form an intricate and multifaceted story. Over the course of the novel, we are taken on a journey by three young 'rubbish boys' who share the main bulk of the storytelling between them. These chapters are interspersed with the first-person accounts of some of the adults who were also affected by the events of the story. Each character brings their own distinct voice and unique perspective, helping to provide a bigger picture of the overall story. Mulligan weaves a large tapestry of storytelling that works to provide rich insights into a fascinating world.

Changing perspectives allows each of the three boys an opportunity to shine. Through their engaging, conversational and matter-of-fact styles of narration, we see the motivations, changes, strengths and doubts of each of the protagonists. Raphael, Gardo and Jun-Jun operate as a team, as reflected in their storytelling relay, happily passing the duties on to each other to present a fair and balanced narrative. After introducing himself and orienting the reader, Raphael announces that he will 'hand on to Gardo after this' and even apologises when he feels he has been monopolising too much of the storytelling, saying, 'Still Raphael. So sorry ... I will hand over.' Later, Gardo tells the reader, 'we agreed to split the story because some things [Raphael] forgets'. Because the boys share the narration, the reader is better able to appreciate each of their unique talents, from Raphael's resilience to Gardo's prudence and Jun-Jun's impressive street smarts. It is worth noting that they write the final chapters together, highlighting their unity and allowing them to take joint credit for their successes, with Jun-Jun proudly declaring that 'the whole point was we did it together'. Mulligan's ingenuity in sharing the narrative duties in this way allows him to give complex and varied voices to the young, the poor and the disenfranchised, positioning his readers to fall in love with his brave and impressive protagonists.

At times, Mulligan shifts the perspective to his adult characters, who provide an interesting contrast to the sometimes naive and narrow worldview of the boys. These trusted and respected elders, namely Father Juilliard and Olivia Weston, also help to corroborate what might be considered a fantastical and unbelievable story. Both become embroiled unwittingly in the boys' adventures, yet instead of providing an enthusiastic recount like Raphael's or Jun-Jun's, they present a more cynical, world-weary point of view. Father Juilliard seems overwhelmed and paralysed by the sheer scale of the poverty he encounters, saying, 'you look around at the thousands who cannot be taken care of and it breaks your heart'. His intimate narration includes a confession of feelings of futility, and he declares that 'it's easy to think what you do in a school like this is of absolutely no consequence or good to anyone'. Olivia reinforces this pessimism, seeing the poverty of Behala as 'an awful punishment that will never end'. She is forced to look injustice directly in the face during her visit to Colva Prison, where the line that 'separates freedom from complete incarceration' is a fine one, easily entrapping the poor and the innocent. Olivia admits to being forever changed by her experiences – 'I learned perhaps more than any university could ever teach me' – sadly acknowledging that what she now understands is that 'the world revolves around money'. Mulligan's adult characters add a crucial layer of understanding to the novel, reminding readers that life is not always a fun adventure, but instead can be a bleak and disheartening endurance test.

Mulligan's compilation of various stories, letters and newspaper clippings helps to paint a picture of widespread corruption. These puzzle pieces fit together to reveal systemic injustice perpetrated by the Vice President, Senator Zapanta. The newspaper excerpts at the end of Part Four reveal perspectives of the wider public, including reports that Zapanta was 'no stranger to controversy … constantly dogged by accusations and scandal' and had 'spirited away thirty million dollars of international aid money'. José Angelico, who saw the politician behind closed doors, notes that his 'smiles are false' and that actually Zapanta was a thief who 'stopped a nation in its tracks'.

Without the benefit of multiple points of view, the fabricated narrative of José Angelico as a criminal could have been his legacy. Yet, thanks to the short chapters from his colleague Grace, and the gravemaker Frederico Gonz, Mulligan reveals José to be a genuine and humble man who was striving to help the poor and hold the powerful to account. Their narrations reveal him to be 'a good man', 'the most trustworthy man', and 'meek and mild'. Although brief, these crucial recollections help reveal the larger story, one of cruelty, corruption and remorselessness.

By using multiple narrators, Mulligan takes his readers on a sprawling and perilous journey from the underclasses of a society to the very upper echelons. Through the shifting, intimate recollections of his three young protagonists, readers become emotionally invested in their wellbeing, relating to and rooting for them as they triumph over evil.

REFERENCES & READING

Text

Mulligan, Andy 2010, *Trash*, Random House, London.

Other resources

Fernandez, Hannah Alcoseba 2022, 'Child scavengers — casualties of the Philippines' war against waste', *Eco-Business*, 4 August, https://eco-business.shorthandstories.com/child-scavengers-casualties-of-the-philippines-war-against-waste/

Harvard Divinity School 2024, 'Catholicism in the Philippines', https://rpl.hds.harvard.edu/faq/catholicism-philippines

Hodal, Kate 2011, 'Living off the landfill: Indonesia's resident scavengers', *The Guardian*, 28 September, https://www.theguardian.com/world/2011/sep/27/indonesia-waste-tip-scavengers

Mulligan, Andy 2015, 'Andy Mulligan: How I wrote *Trash* in 10 days straight', *The Guardian*, 3 February, https://www.theguardian.com/childrens-books-site/2015/feb/03/andy-mulligan-trash-movie-stephen-daldry

Page, Benedicte 2010, 'Blue Peter awards drop "unsuitable" finalist', *The Guardian*, 8 December, https://www.theguardian.com/books/2010/dec/07/blue-peter-awards-drop-finalist-unsuitable